Roots

Insights From The Tree Alphabet Of Old Ireland

~

Olivia Wylie

Introduction

Fogwr gaithi trie flod flescadt
forglas neol,
essa abhai, essnad ealao,
alaind ceoul

The voice of the wind against
the branchy wood
 upon the deep-blue sky: Falls of
the river,
the note of the swan,
Best of all music
-From Lebor Gabála Érenn

Across the British Isles and especially in Ireland, you will find standing stones. They are not as imposing as the great dolmens of Stonehenge, or the mysterious whorl-carved rock of Newgrange. Some of them simply stand in pastures: serene, patient, unconcerned. Sheep crop the grass at their feet. Birds perch on them. You could pass them by, thinking they are natural features, and many do.

But if you take the time, if you stop and look closely, you'll make a discovery. What seemed at first to be random scratchings resolves into a long line, cut with many series of short lines.

You have found an Ogham inscription.

The Ogham, a writing system of the peoples who shared something of a common culture through Britain, Wales, Ireland, Scotland, and the Manx Isles, is many things. It's an alphabet used to write out messages. As early as the second century, stones like the one on the hill of Ballycrovane harbour in Cork proclaimed things as pragmatic as property rights: that stone simply reads 'belonging to Mac Deichet Uí Thorna'. Other Ogham writings are as complex as the people who wrote them, detailing legends and deeds.

Ogham is a mnemonic device used to instruct the student and keep knowledge in circulation. Comprised of four aicmes, or groups, the twenty letters of the Ogham were remembered by the people of Old Ireland much in the same way as we teach our young children their letters today. But rather than 'A is for Apple, B is for Ball', young Irish students learned that 'Beith is for Birch, Luis is for Rowan', as their teacher scratched the lines of each fid, or letter, across a long vertical stave. Read from the bottom of the stave to the top, Ogham asked the reader to begin their understanding at the root of things and work up from there.

These letters were linked to trees the children already knew and interacted with on a daily basis, so the symbols linked to something concrete in their minds and were retained. Even the way a person read was linked to the trees, as the teacher explained the symbols to the student.

The writing and teaching of the Ogham is described in the pages of the 7th century manuscript called the *Auraicept na n-Éces*, The Scholar's Primer:

It e a n-airdi:
deasdruim, tuathdruim, leasdruim,
tredruim, imdruim.
Is amlaid imdreangair crand i
saltrad fora frem in croind ar tus
do lam dess reut, do lam cle fo deoid

These are their signs: right of the
back (back = the stave)
left of the back,
athwart the back,
through the back,
around the back.
It's how one climbs a tree,
treading on the root of the tree
first with your right hand before you
and your left hand after

The symbols also linked to the stories and concepts each tree embodied within the culture, and as such they become a magic as well as a mark. To carve the lines of the ash tree over the door was to invoke the ash tree that weaves harmony between folk. To mark a hazelnut with the lines for *Coll*, the fid for the hazel tree, and carry it was to invite the blessings of all that the hazel tree held: a sharp mind, a keen wit, and a thirst for knowledge. These associations, once ingrained in the mind, allow the user to change themselves through their use of the Ogham. Once you have changed yourself, you begin to change the world around you.

What the Ogham is not, is a divination system. It is an insight system. Though it may tell you where your feet will take you should you continue on the road you tread, the trees are not concerned with the future. They are firmly rooted in the here and now. Do not look to the Ogham to learn your fortune. Look to the Ogham to learn your own heart and the world you are in. Too many of us spend our lives chasing future events and forget to look around at the place we are standing now. The Ogham asks you to stand still and see.

If you are listening, the world has lessons to teach you today. Learn all you can and the future will no longer worry you, for you will know that you have the skills to face what it brings.

The Ogham is a tool for listening to your own heart and the world's whisperings.

As these symbols are deeply tied to the needs and stories of the people who used them, to understand the Ogham you must learn the trees and the tales. In these pages you will be guided through the knowledge each tree has to impart. I often refer to Old Ireland and the Old Irish philosophies, as well as a group of books including the *Book of the Takings of Ireland* and the *Brehon Laws*.

The period is most clearly marked as the era stretching from the building of Newgrange in 3200 BCE to the death of the last high king of Ireland in 1198 CE. The books themselves are mainly recorded between the 4th and 10th centuries, though many sources surviving today are 12th century copies of texts now lost. Archeologists and linguistic scholars agree on this time period as the Old Irish period, having unearthed and translated enough material to give us a clear picture of the social structure that the Ogham grew out of.

During this time, a continuous system of governance existed in Ireland, and extended somewhat through the British Isles: Petty kings–petty from the word *petit*, French for small-ruled kingdoms, elected by their lords and beholden to them. Petty kings owed fealty to a high king who held the power to arbitrate between them all. Nobles cared for their lands in the stead of their king, and held contracts with their tenants and peoples. Fillid taught, recorded history, and instructed through story and song. Durhid kept the calendars of the seasons and oversaw the people's spiritual well-being. Brehon used memorized tracts of law in the form of poems and three-part aphorisms known today as triads to make judgements on disputes and ensure order. Law was focused on recompense rather than punishment: repaying the damage you did was what mattered.Men and women took equal part and equal responsibility at their stations in life, and equal honor was accorded. To harm the honor of another–in modern terms, to cause psychological harm–had the same cost as physical wounding. This system was so ingrained in the people of Ireland that it survived well into the 17th century.

When you see the marks of the Ogham, know that this is the world they are rooted in. That world reaches out to us today in the branches of the trees, grounding us and keeping us steady. Turn the pages, and learn the lessons they offer.

Table of Contents

Begin

Birch

Air gach por a bha 'n an suain,
Bho na thainig fuachd gun bhaigh
Friamhaichidh gach por 's an uir

Every seed that lay in sleep
Since the coming of cold without mercy
Every seed will take root in the earth
-"An Coisrigeadh Sioil," from the
Carmina Gadelica

Botanical names: *Betula pendula*, local American species *Betula papyifera*
Family: Betula
Ogham: Beith
Scots Gaelic: Bher
Irish Gaelic: Beith
Welsh: Bedwyn

Message: Make a beginning.

To begin a thing is to change. Change frightens humanity; as a rule, we've always preferred the world to stay predictable and safely ordered.

A seed is safe and predictable. It is ordered. But it is not alive until it breaks its shell. It is not alive until it begins to try something new.

It is said in the *Book of Ballymote* that Ogham itself began when Ogma, the one it is named for, cut into a birch twig and made a mark to be a message. The story is told in a series of questions and answers:

Whence the Ogham got its name according to sound and matter?
Who are the father and the mother of the Ogham?
By whom it was written?
Not hard.

Ogham is for Ogma in respect to its sound. According to matter, ogum is *og-uaini,* perfect alliteration, which the poets applied to poetry. The father of Ogham is Ogma, the mother of Ogham is his blade. [1]

That first mark made by Ogma's blade, we're told, was the fid of Beith, 'the beginning'. The birch tree bears this mark well; the hints of bright viridian in its canopy are the first sign of spring, welcomed by eyes hungry for color after the dark. In the claw of the robin, so Welsh legend tells us, a birch branch is used to kill the soul of winter in its shape of a wren, and free the world from the cold. [2]

In ecological terms, the birch is known as a pioneer tree. [3] In ground that has been decimated by fire or human action, land that would kill an oak, you will see the valor of birch saplings. Slender and fragile, they raise their branches to the sky and whisper to the wind, "We will grow. We will be a forest someday. We are not afraid."

Beginnings have always frightened humanity. Beginnings and births are perilous, a time of uncertainty as well as joy. Over the years, the birch, has come to be the protector of beginnings to the peoples of northern Europe. In Ireland, birch branches were hung over the beds of women in labor, and in Scotland birch timber cradles protected the new and uncertain lives of infants. In Scandinavia, birch beer was drunk as a spring tonic, and in Wales new couples kissed–and more–under birch boughs to strengthen their union. (4) At Beltane, all across Europe a birch pole or young birch tree became the maypole, heralding the new summer and blessing the beginning of all things that summer would bring. (5)

It is this cheerful valor that the birch tree offers us. "Come on, give it a try." it says in the whisper of wind between its bright leaves, "The worst you can do is learn something."

So many of us let our fears hold us back from trying something new, beginning a venture, taking a plunge. We say, "I'll wait until I'm good enough," "I have bills to pay," "I'm not really ready." We say, "I'll try later." But at the root of all these excuses is the cold little truth. "I'm scared. I think I'll fail. I don't want to be a failure."

Dig out that root as you would dig out a weed, and let the birch tree grow in its place. This is what it will tell you: Sometimes, you are going to make mistakes. Making mistakes is the nature of learning. It is not the nature of failure. The nature of failure is cowardice. You only fail when you stop trying.

Starting something new is terrifying. But do as the birch does: Take a deep breath. Stand quiet and tall. Raise your head up, look forward, and begin.

Bless

Rowan

Ith, blicht, síth, sáma sona,
lína lána, lerthola,
fir ríglaich, co combáid cind
dirmaig forráin

Corn, milk, peace, happy ease,
full nets, ocean's plenty,
Men of worth, amity among
chieftains
-The *Dindshenchas of Carmun*,
11th century

Botanical name: *Sorbus*
Family: Rosaceae
Ogham: Lus
Scots Gaelic: Caorann
Irish Gaelic: Caorthann
Welsh: Criafol

Message: Walk forward, confident in the knowledge that you are part of the pattern. Disharmony is only a passing thing.

Lie down beneath a rowan tree and look up between the branches. Breathe. Watch green and gold leaf shadows spangling the grass around the trunk. Watch the red berries gleaming in the sun, nibbled at by flitting birds. Breathe in the smell of green things growing. And that's when you realize one thing:

Life is good.

The rowan tree is the physical embodiment of this sense of well-being. Sometimes the tree looks so perfect, so beautiful, that it's hard to believe it's real.

Perhaps it truly isn't of this world, the rowan tree. In the Tale of the Wood of Dubhros, it's written that the Tuatha De Danann brought the first rowan berries into the world of men.

"Now the provision the Men of Danu had brought with them from the Land of Promise was crimson nuts, and apples, and sweet-smelling rowan berries. And as they were passing through the district of Ui Fiachrach by the Muaidh, a berry of the rowan tree fell from them, and a young tree grew up from it. And there was virtue in its berries, and no sickness or disease would ever come on any person that would eat them, and those that would eat them would feel the liveliness of wine and the satisfaction of mead in them, and any old person of a hundred years that would eat them would go back to be young again, and any young girl that would eat them would grow to be a flower of beauty." [1]

The rowan tree holds this virtue today, and in its presence no discord and no obstacle can last.

Some say it was the lady Brighid herself who dropped the berry that birthed the first rowan tree [2] and indeed, the rowan is sacred to the lady of the hearth and the smithy, her gift to mankind. The sheer wholesome vitality of rowan is enough to fight off unclean things; rowan berries are tucked in pockets to ward off mischief, untruth and ill intent on the part of man and spirit [3], rowan wood is hung over a cradle to ensure the child is not influenced by evil [4], and rowan berries on the door and window lintels of a home protect against bane and blight entering.

Rowan was used in all the great fire festivals of the Irish: at Imbolg, its red berries were soaked in cream and fed to children and domestic animals to strengthen them. At Beltane, rowan was burned to bless the fertility of the coming harvest and ward off all bane or blight. As the night closed in on Samhain, it was equal armed rowan-wood crosses tied with red thread that protected the folk from the forces of the dark. [4]

When warding off disease, discord and evil, there is no better tree to turn to than the rowan. In the dark and terrible days of winter in northern Europe, tisanes, jams and meads made with rowan berries kept the folk healthy, providing essential supplements of vitamin A and C to ward off scurvy, rickets, and compromised immune systems that led to winter ills. To eat the rowan berries in the dark time of year was "to eat a mouthful of Midsummer." [5]

Rowan is the tree that burns brightest, and we call on it when we most need light. When you look up into the rowan's fine leaves dappled with sunlight, and watch light glint from its carmine berries, you can almost hear it speak. "Life is beautiful," the rowan says in words of dappled light and color, "open your eyes and see it." Its fid in the Ogham, *Lus*, means 'flame' or 'radiance', [6] and in its supple limbs and burning red berries is the pure fire of life. In the light of that fire, all impurity is burned away, and all obstacles are shown to be lessons to help you become greater.

When the rowan is with you, it is time to step out boldly in the certain knowledge that you are part of a pattern, all things in their place and all things blessed.

Shelter

Alder

May I stand
As an island on the marsh
As a hill on the plain
As a tree on the fairy hill
As a star in the moon's waning
As a still sword in the hand
As a child beloved of its ancestors
Bright sights in my eyes
Brave before the host
-From *The poem-book of the Gael*, attributed
to Fionn Mac Cumhaill

Botanical name: *Alnus glutinosa*
Family: Betula
Ogham: Fearn
Scots Gaelic: Feàrna
Irish Gaelic: Fearnóg
Welsh: Gwern

Message: Protect those who are in need.

It seems odd at first glance that the alder is known as *areich fein,* 'shield of the warrior'. But if you were to cut into an alder branch, if you were to watch the white wood redden to the color of blood, you would understand the lesson the alder has to teach: A true warrior is not fierce, unless those they protect are threatened. They are not fighters. They are defenders.

The alder has been named as the tree of defenders since time was time. In ancient days, the hero of Wales, the great poet-warrior Gwydion, stole the three sources of civilization from Arawn, Lord of Death himself, who had jealously guarded them. [1] The wheat sheaf that gave the knowledge of farming, the hound whelp that granted the knowledge of animal husbandry, and the white deer that gave knowledge of woodcraft were brought into the living world and given to humanity, and this sent Arawn into a rage. He rose up in his wrath, ready to lay waste to the entire world and make of it a desert. To keep him out of the living world and defend life itself from annihilation, Gwydion enlisted all the living trees of the wood to be his army and battle against Death beside him. Alder was one of the first to answer the call:

Gwern blaen llin,
A want gysseuin
Helyc a cherdin
Buant hwyr yr vydin.

Alder, front of the line,
formed the vanguard
Willow and Rowan
were late to the fray. [2]

Gwydion chose to carry alder as his standard, and in the battle could be recognized by the gleaming branches he bore. That day, he defended life using two sets of weapons: the weapons of the battlefield and the weapons of the clever mind. And with the help of the trees, he rode to victory that day. By the strength of the trees, Death was driven back and Life was defended.

In the home and the hearth, alder wood is the wood of protection and resistance to evil influences. Liking water and extremely resistant to decay, alder trees were planted to create natural protections on the banks of dikes and water courses. Alder wood was used in any place where wood would be under constant attack and need strength: in the water wheels that ground the people's grain, in bowls and utensils for the kitchen, in the pilings of docks and the making of boats and fishing gear. [3] Alder twigs were woven into fish traps called weirs, and wooden cobbles for roads were made from alder timber. [4] In Wales and southern Ireland, all milk was contained in alder churns. Alder wood kept the milk fresh longer due to its antiseptic properties, which protected the household from financial loss and foodborne illness in a place and time when milk was a staple. [5]

Alder is also a healer of injury: its boiled bark could be used to wash and staunch the blood of deep wounds. [6]

Symbolically, alder is the tree of the defender. The defender does not seek battle, but they will not let injustice run rampant. Laurie sums it up best: "The warrior protects what is loved, and the container protects what is held within it." [7]

When the alder speaks, this is what they say: "You are strong today. Defend those who are weak when you are strong. Take up your weapon in the defense of those in need, whatever your weapon is. Raise your hand, raise your voice, raise your pen to quell evil and defend the folk. The people around you are your tribe, and you must care for them as they care for you. That is your duty."

Attend

Willow

An losíc saileach uasal sruthán,
fid deimin na nualan;
Beich na bèith an deol,
Miam caiach in cró caim.

The noble willow burn not, a tree sacred to poems;
Within his bloom bees are drinking,
all love the little shelter.
-Excerpt, "The Song of the Forest Trees" from the
Silva Gadelica [1]

Botanical name: *Salix alba*
(and about three hundred other species)
Family: Salix
Ogham: Saille
Scots Gaelic: Seilich
Irish Gaelic: Saileich
Welsh: Helyg
French: Saule

Message: Pay attention to what's around you; there's more going on than you think.

Quiet, rippling water. It's one of the most soothing sounds you can experience. It isn't so silent as to induce anxiety, nor is it so loud as to distract. The sound of quiet water invites us, in turn, to grow quiet. The water allows the mind to cease its scurrying, grow still, relax and expand.

Above the water, there will be willow leaves whispering.

The willow is a graceful tree. It retains its charm throughout its life, growing from lithe youth to aged and gracious dowager of the wood. Its down-hanging branches and wide, shallow root system by the water's edge often conspire to create hidden seats, nooks and crannies custom-made for the protection of the contemplative, and the sharing of confidences. Under the willow tree, you have the peace and the time to look at the world as it truly is. And, perhaps, to look at your own soul as well.

It's all too easy to become so wrapped up in your own thoughts, your own goals, your own views, that you stop seeing the world as it is and see it only as you expect it to be. Some people go through their entire life like this, seeing the world and all its happenings only as they impact themselves. They've forgotten that they are only a part of a vast pattern. The willow is the tree of patterns: the patterns of leaves on water, the patterns in the notes of the harp, the patterns of weaving notes and weaving branches.

The willow, for its flexible durability, has always been a favorite for weaving. Willow branches have been used in the creation of all things in the pattern of a life: fences and baskets, cradles and caskets in Scotland and Ireland, [2] wattle and daub walls and fences in Britain. [3] Remains of willow-woven walls have been found dating back to Neolithic times. [4] Wickerwork furniture is nearly as old. [5] The tree has woven itself even into our languages: the root words for willow, wicket, wicker, and wick (a rural

14

English term for 'pliable' and often a synonym for 'alive' as it referenced bendable live twigs, still used in Yorkshire today) [6] is the Anglo-Saxon 'wic', which translates directly as 'to bend'. It is also the root word of the English word 'witch', which meant 'one who bends, one who manipulates.' Linguistically, the work of a witch was, quite literally, the work of bending, changing, and creating patterns. This term may later have gained an entire wagon train of baggage, but at its linguistic root it simply meant: one who changes. One who bends. [7]

If you think about it, this is the greatest power: to be able to change the world around you, yes, but even more so to be flexible enough to change yourself. A person who can see clearly and think flexibly is one who can do well wherever they are. Those who can't will suffer. It may be as simple as a nasty scare in traffic caused by your own inattention, tripping over a crack in the sidewalk while your mind was elsewhere. Or it could be as terrible as the lie that eats you inside: the lie you've been told, the lie you've been telling yourself. Refusing to look the world in the eye and admit an unpleasant truth to yourself is perhaps the worst type of self-inflicted blindness, a toxic condition named in Irish as *an galar rúnach*, a malady of secrets.

A great king once learned this truth to his shame, and the willow tree taught him his lesson. In old Ireland, a physical imperfection was a sign that a king was unfit to rule, but that was nothing to the blemish of the lie on the soul of Labhraidh Loingseach. Brian O'Sullivan tells the tale like this:

Labhraidh Loingseach was said to have had horse's ears. He kept this secret by growing his hair long, having it cut once a year and then putting the barber to death.

One day when a widow's only son was chosen for the unpopular job of cutting the king's hair, the widow begged the king not to kill him. Moved, Labhraidh Loingseach agreed on the condition that the barber never tell a living person of his secret.

The burden of the secret weighed so heavily on the widow's son that after a time he took ill. On the advice of a druid, he released himself of the secret by whispering it into the bowl of a great willow. Divested of the burden, he soon became well again.

Sometime later, Labhraidh Loingseach's harpist broke his instrument and made a new harp out of the very willow the widow's son had passed the secret to. One night, during a great feast at Labhraidh Loingseach's hall, he started to play and suddenly the harp sang:

> *Dá chluais chapaill ar Labhraidh Loingseach!*
> Two horse's ears on Labhraidh Loingseach! [8]

As the story shows, a lie will sicken us, especially the one we tell ourselves. And the truth will not be denied. Someday, we will have to face it. Better to do so willingly than be forced into it, don't you think?

It may have been the lilting sound of the willow's leaves and the rippling water that inspired harpists in the ancient Ireland to prefer it as the wood for their harps. [9] The soft sound of a harp is indeed kin to the sound of moving water: lilting, rolling, inviting thought and contemplation. True stillness and contemplation is something we sometimes lose track of in the modern world, but it was the cornerstone of knowledge among the Irish fili, the Welsh bardd, and their nobles as well. When asked what boyhood habits allowed him to grow into a splendid man, the great king Cormac Mac Art answered with this:

> "Not hard to tell
> I was a listener in woods
> I was a gazer at stars
> I was blind where secrets were concerned
> I was silent in a wilderness
> I was talkative among many" [10]

In the quiet, in gazing at the stars, in contemplation, you start seeing the things you've been missing. In spring you will notice the tiny willow flowers, which the bees have already found. You see the world around you for what it really is, not the blurred background your busy mind has made of it. You begin, if you sit still long enough, to notice things. And in paying attention, *really* paying attention, you may begin to learn.

Listen. The willow is whispering. If you're quiet, you'll hear the words.

> "Sit still.
> Calm down.
> Open your eyes.
> See what's really there.
> Now. Keep your eyes open. Keep looking.
> Don't go back to sleep."

Connect

Ash

*Trí bannaí a cheangal dúinn le saol
onórach:
An banna an cairdeas
an banna an teaghlaigh
an banna an fine.*

Three bonds that tie us to an honorable
life:
The bond of friendship,
the bond of family,
the bond of the clan.
-Written by Giolla Íosa Mór Mac
Fhirbhisigh, from the *Leabhar Buidhe
Leacáin*

Botanical names: *Fraxinus excelsior*, local American species *Fraxinus americana*
Family: Oleaceae
Ogham: Nuin
Scots Gaelic: Uinnseann
Irish Gaelic: Fuinseog
Welsh: Ynn

Message: Our strength is in our bonds to one another.

When the ash tree leafs out, I know that summer is finally on its way. Ash is the tree that children play under on May afternoons. The weavers once set their looms hanging from the ash tree to take advantage of the shade, chatting as they twisted warp and woof together. It was the ash bark that dyed their cloth blue and green, the shade of the leaves that encouraged steady work and seamless talk. Because of its resilience, ash was in fact the favorite wood for making into the looms that would weave the baby's blanket, the bride's dress and the grandmother's shroud. [1]

In the summer, it's the tree people gather beneath to sit and talk. In the winter, it's the ash logs that will burn long enough for many stories by the fire, for it burns longest and warmest. [2] In all its forms, the ash is the tree that convinces us to sit down for the long, leisurely conversations that weave us into one another's lives. The topic of the conversation rarely matters. It's the conversation that draws us close.

When we find the right people to sit with in the leafy shade and while away the hours, we feel an overwhelming sense of well-being. We are among our people, our tribe, and we are connected. This connection is vital to our survival. When we are in healthy social situations, studies have shown that we think faster, have elevated levels of the 'feel good' chemicals in our brains, and are healthier overall. [3] It has been proven that people suffering from loneliness actually die at a higher rate. [4]

Why?

Because cooperating was what let our most ancient ancestors survive. Other creatures grew great teeth, claws, horns or legs with staggering speed. Humans? We grew connections to one another. Together, a clan could achieve what no one person could. So we banded together, and the more we cooperated, the more complex our brains became. [5] The more social we were, the stronger we grew. Alone, we suffered.

The truth of connection is enshrined even in laws dating back as far as the art of writing takes us. Under Brehon law, all householders had some obligation to provide hospitality. To refuse was to pay a heavy social price: loss both of property and of honor. [6] In a small agricultural community, 'honor' was not a nebulous thing. It was, in effect, your social credit. Prove that you served poor fare at your table, and you'd have no one sitting there to help you bring your harvests in. Prove that you were untrustworthy, and you would be left out of all social contracts. To lose your honor among the clan was to suffer.

In story, it was a staff of ash wood that embodied this spirit of social obligation, both good and ill. In the *Yellow Book of Lecan*, we're told the story of The Ash Staff held in the hand of the Dagda, wisest among the Tuatha Dé Danann. [7]

When his young son had fallen in battle and the Dagda was in mourning, he wandered the island in a daze, carrying the body in search of a way to restore his boy. Alone and in sorrow on the road, the boy's body a shrouded hump upon his back, the great man met three brothers arranged around their fire.

"What is the news?" he asked, politely gesturing in request for a seat by the fire, but one of the brothers held up a threatening staff. The other two clutched the things they held close.

"We are three sons of one father and one mother," the eldest snapped rudely, "and the treasures of our father are shared among us."

"What have you there?" the Dagda asked, maintaining his good manners as best he could.

"The great staff that you see," said the eldest, "a smooth tip and a rough tip it has. A gentle end here and a violent end there it has. One end kills the living, and the other end restores to life the dead."

"What of the shirt and shield," said the Dagda, "what are their values?"

"He that takes on himself the cloak, his choice of shape, and his choice of coloring, while it is on him. The shirt then, he'll have no grief, nor any sickness, while it is on him. Now get away with you." And the brothers turned the guest from their fire with sneers.

Now, the Dagda might have grabbed the shirt and shed his grief. But instead, he snatched the staff of bright ash wood, and touched each of the three brothers with its rough end. Dead, they fell to the earth. Then the Dagda unwrapped his son and touched him with the smooth and shining tip, and he started to life.

"Who are the three dead here before me?" said Cermad.

"Three who I met," said the Dagda, "and the treasures of their father were with them for dividing. They gave the loan of the staff to me, and I killed them with the rough end, and restored you to life with the smooth end."

"Misfortune in doing that," said Cermad, "when that which restored me to life did not restore them to life as well."

And the Dagda knew his son was wiser than he. The men had paid the price for breaking the law of hospitality, which is death. But Cermad had seen it fit to offer kindness to strangers, which is to offer life.

Together, father and son touched the three men with the smooth tip of the ash staff, and they lived again.

When we stop offering kindness to one another, we lose our humanity. When we cease communicating as equals and as part of a community, we lose an integral part of ourselves.

When we sit under the ash tree, she bends her branches over us and whispers:

"Every one of you is a bright thread. But the cloth is stronger when the weave is tight.
Talk to one another.
Listen to one another.
Help one another.
This is how the fabric of life is woven."

Beware

Hawthorn

Trí fáilti ata messu brón:
fáilti fir íar ndiupairt,
fáilti fir íar luga eithig,
fáilti fir íar fingail.

Three rejoicings that are worse than sorrow:
the joy of a man who has defrauded another,
the joy of a man who has perjured himself,
the joy of a man who has slain his own brother.
-From the *Book of Húi Maine*

Botanical name: *Crataegus monogyna*
Family: Ericaceae
Ogham: Huath
Scots Gaelic: Sgitheach
Irish Gaelic: Sgitheach
Welsh: Y ddraenen wen
French: Aubépine

Message: Be aware of the dangers around you. Discern the truth from the lie.

At the edge of the field, stark against the wide blue sky, a lone tree guards the gate. It casts no wide shadow, for it is only a little taller than a man. It does not seem a great thing. But brush past this tree at your peril; already its thorns are dyed with blood and adorned with scraps of cloth, bits of hair. Disrespect the hawthorn, and it will exact its price.

The English word for the tree, 'hawthorn', comes from an older Saxon word, 'haegthorn' meaning hedge-thorn. [1] It is the hedge that guards and warns.

Hawthorn guards the boundaries between many things: between men's lands when it stretches in thorny hedges between fields throughout the British Isles, [2] between the seasons when its flowering marks the true end of winter, [3] and between the worlds of men and sidhe, when it stands guard over fairy raths and homes.

Hawthorn trees were, and still are, known as fairy trees. They were thought to have magical properties and were often left uncut, even if hedges were being removed. [4]

The fairy tree is easily recognized: it stands alone on a hilltop or in a dell. Often it has been tied with clootie ribbons and bits of cloth enclosing entreaties. The man who would cut such a tree shows either culpable stupidity or willful blindness, and he will pay for it. There are tales of what happens to the man who cuts a fairy tree, none of them pleasant, but many of them recent.

According to the Irish Times, a multi-million dollar roadway project was re-routed in 1999 to respect a particular fairy thorn of County Clare. The article reads, "There had even been a warning from a folklorist of a curse on the new roadway and of motoring fatalities if the fairy bush was to fall victim to the £100 million plan to bypass Newmarket-on-Fergus and Ennis." A famed local storyteller had given the warning in no uncertain terms. The article continues, "Yesterday, the county engineer, Mr Tom Carey, confirmed that after surveying the fairy thorn bush in the detailed plans and drawings prepared, the council has found that it would now be able to incorporate the "sceach" into the proposed bypass." [5]

This move on the part of the county is wise indeed, considering what happened to a man who was not so respectful. As Mara Freeman writes it, "Earlier in this century, a construction firm ordered the felling of a fairy thorn on a building site in Downpatrick, Ulster. The foreman had to do the deed himself, as all of his workers refused. When he dug up the root, hundreds of white mice–supposed to be the faeries themselves–ran out, and while the foreman was carting away the soil in a barrow, a nearby horse shied, crushing him against a wall and resulting in the loss of one of his legs." [6]

Older tales tell of even greater costs: death of yourself, your livestock, or perhaps worst of all, loss of your easy sleep, so that you would be restless all your nights. [7]

But what caused all these harms? Why the cost for harming the hawthorn?

It is the cost of ignoring the warnings life has given you. One may refuse to see the troubles in their life for many reasons: greed, willfulness, fear of what will change when they face the truth, love of the lie they've been told or have been telling.

But the refusal will only bring on heartbreak, all the worse because it was self-made. It is the shot in the dark, the scream in the night. In our modern world, this is the symbol of the bug that shuts down your computer and the bill you weren't expecting. It's the car that you don't see which hits you. Huath is the moment when you slam on the brakes, knowing it's already too late. This is the fid of the painful surprise, brought on by your lack of awareness.

Even great heroes learn the hawthorn's lesson, to their cost.

As it is recounted in the *Táin Bó Cúailnge*, the great hero Cuchulainn was called into a battle that had no good cause and no hope of success. But he had his honor to uphold, and so he prepared himself.

He had warning against the road he chose. When his mother handed him the blessing cup, he found the mead was turned to blood. Three times his mother filled the cup, and three times it was bloody.

Three times Cuchulainn set to put his horse, the Grey of Macha, in her chariot traces that day. Twice she refused. On the third attempt, she cried blood. But Cuchulainn was determined to go to battle.

Even when he met three crones cooking a hound on a hawthorn spit, Cuchulainn would not heed the warning of his namesake, the hound, dead upon the spit.

That was the day Cuchulainn died.

To sit beneath a hawthorn is no bad thing. White-flowered in the spring and ruby-berried in the fall, it is as beautiful and as dangerous as life itself. If you listen, this is what she tells you.

"Have a care. The things you do not see will do you much harm. The truths you refuse to see will be your undoing. Be aware. Have a care."

Understand

Oak

Cetheora aipgitre gáise:
ainmne, sonmathe, sobraide,
sothnges;
ar is gáeth cach ainmnetach,
sái cach somnath,
fairsing cach sobraid,
sochoisc cach sothengtha

Four elements of wisdom:
patience, quietness, sobriety, well-spokenness;
for every patient person is wise, every quiet person is a sage,
every sober person is generous, every well-spoken person is good
company
-From *The Yellow Book of Lecan*

Botanical name: *Quercus robur*
Family: Fagaceae
Ogham: Dair
Scots Gaelic: Daraich
Irish Gaelic: Dair
Welsh: Derw
French: Chêne

Message: Do not shout your convictions aloud. Stand by them every day. That speaks more loudly.

Under the oaks, the acorns are falling. The light is gold. Beneath the great boughs, there abides a deep serenity.

The oak brought the peoples of northern Europe a sense of peace in the autumn, when a rich harvest of acorns made bountiful flour to feed the folk and good grazing to fatten the pigs. [1] Since it was said that the serving of pig meat at the table was 'the freeing of shame from every face', [2] a good acorn harvest presaged a good winter.

On a deeper level, oak trees bring us calm by their very presence. German experiments have shown that the blood pressure of tourists visiting a forest rises under conifers. But under a stand of oaks, the tourists' blood pressure falls below pre-experimental levels, growing peaceful. [3]

In summer the wood of the oak is cut to make many things, for it lasts longest. Indeed, a single oak lives an average of six hundred years. Some have been found that have reached a millennium, [4] and archeological digs have unearthed oaken artifacts dating to 8,000 years of age [5]. Oak was the preferred wood for doors, casks and all things that would be subject to the punishment of the elements. It was also the wood of choice for objects that were intended to be passed down from one generation to the next. As Erynn Laurie writes, "the tree itself is long lived and working its wood takes effort, but what is made from it is frequently exquisite in craftsmanship and long lasting, for less talented craftsmen use softer woods to practice their arts, graduating to harder and more valuable woods as their skill grows." [6]

This toughness is engendered by both the growth habits and the biochemistry of the species. Under a microscope, a cross-section of oak wood is shown to have many tiny, closely spaced cells. This means that the tree lays down new growth very slowly, but it can withstand both intense pressure and damage since its wood is extremely dense: the average density is about 0.75 g/cm3 (0.43 oz/cu in). [7] These cramped cells also make invasion by bacteria more difficult. And if bacteria does happen to find a way in through a wound, the extremely high level of tannic acid in the tree's sap is sure to kill it off. [8] Our ancestors were right: Oak is the tree of permanence.

So long-lived is the oak, and so tall, that it has been associated with kingship and the gathering of great wisdom. Across the landscape of northern Europe, place names tell us what the tree meant to the people, for so many place names include 'Derry' or 'Dare', Anglicizations of 'daire', the word for the oak. Kildare, 'church of the Oak,' Derrybeg, 'the Little Oak Wood', Derrydorragh the 'dark oak wood' and Derry itself, 'Place of the Oak', are all examples. [9] As the oak remembers time, people remember the oak.

People once called themselves after the oaks as well as their places; there were tribes in the 11th century known as 'men of the oaks', [10] and in times older than that, the priestly class themselves were called 'Dur-wid', which can be translated as 'wise as oak trees' or 'those with the knowledge of the oak'. [11] For centuries, the druids led the folk and venerated the oak as the ever-living tree, source of vitality.

As it was associated with the land and wisdom of the land, so the oak was associated with sovereignty and the wise rulership of kings. Called 'The Tara of the Wood', [12] the oak was the tree of the Dagda, father of the Gods, whose great strength lay in his endurance. No matter what befell, the Dagda would stand firm for his people.

There is a tale in *The Book of Invasions* that tells us of the Dagda and his steadfast way. It had come the time of Samhain during the seven years of strife between the terrible Formorii and the Tuatha de Dannan, and a truce had been called for the holiday. Under the name of the truce, the Formorii invited the Dagda to a feast at their camp. Since it was a great offense to refuse the hospitality of a host and a greater one to refuse the food of a host, the Dagda accepted.
When he reached the encampment, he found that the Formorii had set a trap for him; a pit had been dug and filled with eighty cauldrons worth of oats, milk and honey. Now the Dagda was great and formidable, but this was more food than fifty warriors could take up. And yet it was Samhain, and to refuse the food of a host would be a crime. So the Dagda took up a great spoon. The Formorii snickered. And the Dagda ate, and ate, until he was scraping the base of the pit. The Formorii stared in shock.

"But you have left some porridge behind," said one of the enemy querulously.

Hearing this, the Dagda scooped a great spoonful of rock and dirt into his mouth. Then he stood, dusted off his jerkin, and left the enemy camp triumphant.

When the world is daunting, tuck an acorn in your pocket. Each time you touch it, remember the strength of the oak. If you have made your judgements well, there is wisdom in waiting out the braggards and the bluster. If you are firm in your convictions, you have no need to shout them. You have only to stand by them

Craft

Holly

Trí duirn ata dech for bith:
dorn degsáir,
dorn degmná,
dorn deggobann

Three hands that are best in the world:
the hand of a good carpenter,
the hand of a skilled woman,
the hand of a good smith
-From *The Book Of Ballymote*

Botanical name: *Illex aquifolium*
Family: Aquifoliaceae
Ogham: Tinne
Scots Gaelic: Cuileann
Irish Gaelic: Cuileann
Welsh: Celyn
French: Houx

Message: Kindle your fire. Pick up the tools of your trade and begin the work.

The land is white. The sky is grey. Warmth is the distant dream of a fool.

And then your eyes catch red fire. The berries shine like hot coals fallen in the snow. The color of the leaves makes eyes that have seen gloom too long shine again.

Wandering in the dead of winter, you have found the holly tree.

However bitter the cold grows, holly is the fire that still burns bright. In the darkest times, it recalls us to life. It's no wonder that it was held in high esteem throughout the lands of northern Europe. Even today we remember this in our Yuletide songs; don't we still sing:

Deck the Halls with Boughs of Holly [1]

And even more tellingly,

Of all the trees that are in the wood, the Holly bears the Crown [2]

In the Ogham, the fid of holly is *Tinne,* and it shares a root word with 'tine', the modern Irish word for fire. Other names for this fid include *tinne iarn,* an ingot or bar of iron, and *trian ni-airm,* one third of a tool. [3] Like so many things in the ancient landscape, the tree earned these names through deeds, and holly earned hers in the forge.

30

To the ancient Irish blacksmith at his work, the holly was the best of all woods. In the *Silva Gadelica* it is written:

cuilenn loisc a úr . cuilenn loisc a críon i   *Holly, burn it green; holly, burn it dry;*
gach crann ar bith becht cuilenn as dech díob!   *Of all trees the most esteemed is holly!* [4]

These lines refer to traits inherent in the holly's morphology and the qualities it imparts. A tough shrub or small tree of 30 feet in the wild, holly was an excellent source of fine grained hardwood that created excellent charcoal without the need for lengthy seasoning. Though it contains saponins, it neither produces noxious smoke nor bursts due to high moisture content when dropped fresh into the fire. [5] This made it invaluable to a smith, especially one who might need fresh wood in a hurry should a battle come up and many new weapons be needed. Holly charcoal was specifically valued for the long, sustained heat required to create and repair iron and steel tools. The wood of the female holly was preferred, for her bright red berries were seen as a source of vitality. It was seen as so valuable that in one law tract, it was required that every landowner keep holly charcoal by for the repair of weapons. [6] Holly wood came to the smith's hand as they created weapons and tools as well: its tough, springy wood was perfect for the axles of chariots, the spokes of wheels and the shafts of axes and spears. Hence, it earned the name *trian ni-airm,* for it made one third of a tool, the center or the shaft. Sitting at the right hand of the smith, holly became linked to the art of the forge and the fire of creation.

In the smith's forge, matter is transformed with hard work and skill from one state to another. Ore becomes metal. Pig iron becomes steel. Some people call this magic, but magic in the English language implies an easy wave of hands and things coming with no effort. Better to use the Irish way of speaking of these changes: as an art. An art is not quick nor easy. An art takes great time and great effort to master. The artist crafts themselves as much as they craft their work, fighting to gain skills, making mistakes and learning, working every day to become something better than they were.

The work is daunting. But the fruits of the labor are worth the effort.

In today's world, we've separated the body of an art or a craft from the soul. We separate the work of the world into work for artists, who we see as flighty creatures with flamboyant dreams, and work for hard-headed people who do the dirty work. But in older times, there was an art to all things. There was an art to making tools. There was an art to making weapons, an art to war, an art to building a wall. That did not mean it was not hot, heavy, dirty and difficult work. It was. But here's the key: to the people doing it, the work was seen as a form of art. The people who saw the world in this way created tools for daily life that were both functional and beautiful, both strong and pleasing. And the 'artist' was no more or less valuable than the 'warrior' when trouble came calling.

When true sorrow came over the land of Ireland in the days of the legends, it was craftsmen, not warriors, who were the midwives of victory.

The Book of Invasions tells us that the darkest days to come upon Ireland were not during the first great battle between the blessed children of Danú and their terrible foes, the Formorii, for the soul of the land. It was in the time between the first battle and the second, when a false king sat on the throne at Tara. The renowned leader, Nuada, had lost his throne in the first battle of Mag Turied by losing his hand, for the law held that only a man whole in body could sit on the throne of the high king and embody the health of the land. Bres, who took his throne, might have been whole in body, but he was hollow of spirit, and the land grew sorry and sour under his reign. He was cast from his throne by the curse of a bard and good riddance to him, but Nuada was yet denied the throne by his wound, though his folk needed his guidance.

In his forge, the smith Goibniu, greatest in his trade, decided to make all well. He fetched a man of equal rank in his own art, the great healer Dian Cécht. Together they worked seven days and seven nights, and at the end of it, Nuada bore a shining silver hand that worked as well as the one he was born with. Whole again, the high king regained his rightful place. In time, his people were strong enough to face the Formorii again.

On that great day, Nuada named Lugh the All Crafted as his battle leader. As his men gathered, Lugh asked each of them what power they wielded. When Goibniu was asked what his strength in battle would be, this was his answer:

"For every spear that separates from its shaft or sword that breaks in battle, I will provide a new weapon in its place. No spearpoint which my hand forges will make a missing cast. No skin which it pierces will taste life afterward." [8]

In the smith's words there is a lesson: The world needs great warriors and leaders, but just as dearly it needs craftsmen who work their art with passion and skill. Do not count your art as less valuable than another's because it is of a different kind. Without Goibniu at his forge, the De Danann warrior in the fray is dead. Give equal glory to the fighter and the healer, to those who craft and those who rule. Without the artist's skill and the craftsman's dedication, the king would not sit upon his throne.

The tools of your art could be anything. A pen. A fiddle. A keyboard. A shovel. A knife. Holly doesn't care what the shape of the tool is. She only urges that you pick it up and get to work crafting yourself and your arts.

The world needs your skill, holly insists, poking at you with prickly leaves.

"So go on." she whispers, "Kindle the fire. Pick up the tools. Get to work."

Learn

Hazel

A question, clever lad. Whence have you come?

Not hard to answer:
I spring from the heel of a wise man,
From the meeting-place of knowledge,
From the place where goodness dwells;
From the red sunrise I come,
Where grow the nine hazels of poetic art,
From the splendid circuits in a land
Where truth is measured by excellence
Where falsehood fades,
Where there are many colours,
Where poets are refreshed
-From "The Colloquy of the Two Sages", the *Book of Leinster*

Botanical name: *Corylus avellana*
Family: Betulaceae
Ogham: Coll
Scots Gaelic: Calltainn
Irish Gaelic: Coll
Welsh: Cyll
French: Noisette

Message: Follow your curiosity. Never stop learning.

There is a place where water reflects a tapestry of green light. The pool gurgles to itself in the shade of nine hazel trees. If you watch, you may see the flash of a salmon's fin breaking the water.

There! Did you see it?

They say that fish bears the name of Knowledge, and he is not easily caught. But he is worth the chase.

In the Brehon law, the hazel is listed among the Nobles of the Wood, which may seem odd to a casual observer: hazel trees are not imposing. Full-grown trees rarely reach over 30 feet, and could often be described as shrubs. Many common hazels grow only 8 or 9 feet high. [1] But the casual observer did not live in the 6th, 7th, and 8th century, when hazelnuts were one of the most important staple foods throughout the Celtic world. Nutritionally, the nuts are impressive: a 100 gram serving provides 18 grams of protein, 50 grams of LDL fat, and all the calcium a grown person needs. [2] Add that to the fact that hazelnuts stored well, and you begin to understand their importance.

34

Archeological evidence shows that the Celtic peoples were harvesting hazelnuts on an industrial scale as far back as the Mesolithic era. At sites in Farnham in England's Surrey county, at Cass ny Hawin on the Isle of Man, and on the island of Colonsay in Scotland, shallow pits have been found filled with hundreds of thousands of burned hazelnut shells, accompanied by fire pits and storage chambers. Those in Colonsay have been dated at nine thousand years old. [3]

The poetry of the people reflects the proof the land offers up. A recurrent compliment for a land or a tribe was the worth of its hazel trees. In the 11th century tale, *The Guesting of Athirne*, we are told of the joys of autumn in the words:

"the hard ground is covered with heavy fruit
Hazel-nuts of good crop
fall from great old trees on the dikes" [4]

Other reflections are seen in such expressions as "*Doire nath* on which fair nutted hazels are constantly found," and "O'Berga, the chief for whom the hazels stoop," [5] which are peppered throughout the lineages of kingdoms and the recordings of the lines of kings in all the manuscripts available today.

Often hazel and oak are mentioned in the same legend or poem, and there is a logic to this: the two trees were viewed as the two forms of knowing. In the Irish language, there are two separate words for two separate types of knowing: *eagna*, the wisdom of experience, and *imbas*, the spark of new ideas and the thirst for knowledge. [6] The nuts of the two trees embody the difference. Both oak and hazel trees produce nuts in plenty, but while acorns require much processing to become edible, hazelnuts need only be cracked open at the right time. The truths of the oak are bone-deep wisdoms, and those who take the oak's way were *droi-vid*, wise as the oaks.

Knowledge of today and the search for it belonged to the *fillid*, or poet, and their tree is the hazel. The *fillid* of the legends held not wisdom but *imbas*, usually translated as inspiration. We're told in the tale of "The Colloquy of Ancients" from *The Book of Leinster* that the place for the aged sage is among the oak trees, but the place for the clever young folk who served in the warrior band of the Fianna was the hazel grove, and their food was hazelnuts. [7]

It is fitting that Finn would want to feed his warriors on hazelnuts, for legend tells us that is where he gained his own abilities as a genius and a general. In the 12th century manuscript *Macgnimartha Fionn*, The Boyhood Deeds of Fionn, we're told that the poet Finegas found a secret pool beneath nine hazel trees at the head of the Boyne river, and realized that he'd come upon the *Tobar Segais*, the Well of Knowledge. In the water a single salmon swam, fat with the hazelnuts he'd eaten. Finegas knew that the man who tasted the salmon's flesh would know all there was to know in the world, and he spent seven years in hunting it. But it was his new servant boy Finn who cooked it, Finn who burned his thumb on hot fish grease and unwisely stuck his burnt thumb in his mouth, and Finn who gained the knowledge. At times it's the student, not the master, who makes the great leap in understanding. The student, you see, has not learned what is impossible.

But Finegas would not have found the pool, and Finn would not have gained his knowledge if someone before them had not dared to take the first step.

There is an older story in the hazel pool. It is the story of curiosity.

In the *Dindsenchas* we read that there was a time when no imbas existed in the world, save in a single pool. High King Nechtan had entrapped all knowledge and all inspiration in a pool beneath nine hazel trees, and had a great well cover fitted over it. Every person who wanted to lead or tell tales had to pay Nechtan three rods of gold, three rods of silver, and three years of servitude for one sip from the well. Soon Nechtan grew wealthy, and his wealth bought him the friendship of a lord with a beautiful daughter. She was called Boann of the Fair Face, and she went to the court of Nechtan as his bride.

At first Boann was happy. But her husband's stinginess upset her. In Nechtan's court, the scraps of the table went to the pigs rather than the poor, and his harpers sang dull songs; even they were not given a taste from the Well of Knowledge.

"Husband," she said, "Could we not give more? We have so much."

"Hush woman," Nechtan barked, "do you see to the kitchens."

For a time Boann was content. Since there was little for her to do, each day she went walking. In time she found a path barred by three spears; the path to the hazel pool.

"Husband," she said, "May I see the hazel pool? I have heard of its beauty."

"Hush woman," said Nechtan, "Only I and three cupbearers may go near the pool. It is death to all others. Do you go and see to your loom."

Now Boann was incised. She was of no use in the court, but the people thought her too great to let her roll up her sleeves and aid in the daily work of the town. And if she heard 'hush woman' once more she'd shriek like the bean-sidhe.

It was coming time for the great Midsummer fair in Nechtan's land, and he as king would be presiding. Boann went to him.

"Husband," she said, "I would go to the fair."

"Hush woman!" cried Nechtan. "Do you stay here and see to your weaving. I will be back in three days or so."

He rode out.

Boann pulled on her mantle and walked into the forest. Soon, she came to a place where nine hazel trees drooped over a great well covering set in the earth.

Boann stepped beneath the trees. She opened the hatch in the well cover, dipped in her hands and drank.

For three days Boann sat by the hazel pool, ate the nuts, drank the water, and learned. On the third day she acted. Walking three times counterclockwise around the pool, she broke the enchantment laid over the waters within. The well covering burst and the water that had been trapped so long bubbled out, and Boann laughed as it flowed out into a stream, then a river, and she ran beside it as it grew. The running stream was passing Nechtan's castle as he came riding up.

"Woman!" he cried, "What have you done to my well?"

"It was never your well to claim, Nechtan!" she called in reply as she ran.

"Wife, come back!" he roared.

"I am not your wife. You treated me as none, and so I am none to you," she called over her shoulder, and ran on. He spurred his horse after her, but she became an otter and leapt into the water.

The river flowed on, down to the sea. It soaked into the land and fed the crops. It became rain and fell in all places.

Today the Boyne river still flows, and there is imbas in all things and all places. We have only to dive in and go looking for it.

Persevere

Apple

A abhall, abhlachóg,
Tren rotchraithenn cách

O apple tree, little apple tree,
Much art thou shaken
-"An Laoi Shuibhne," 12th century
rhyme

Botanical name: *Malus sylvestris*
Family: Pyrus, malus
Ogham: Ceirt
Scots Gaelic: Crann Ubhall, ubhal-fiadhaich, Cuirt
Irish Gaelic: Crann Úll, Aball
Welsh: Afallen; pren afalau, Afal

Message: Persevere through the hard times.

Here in Colorado, the apple is one of the first trees to bloom. It often suffers for its enthusiasm, broken again and again by the last and heaviest of the winter snows just as it shows its beauty. I've seen wild apple trees lose more than three quarters of their branches, cracked and broken under the weight of the crushing snow.

But then something amazing happens. The tree sends up whippy shoots from the broken places. It looks ridiculous, a tree with cracked branches and whippy suckers all over it. But if you cut away the old, dead branches and let a few of the suckers grow, you'll soon see sturdy new branches working to replace what was lost. If the tree must be cut down altogether, just wait. Soon you'll see a handful of suckers rise from the stump. Choose the strongest of them, thin the rest out, and in a few years a new tree stands where the old did, blossoms on its branches.

The Ogham linked to the apple tree isn't actually 'apple', *aball,* but *ceirt*, 'rag'. [1] Erynn Laurie and Ellen Hopman both link this name in their books to the old tradition of tying 'clootie rags' (clootie being a bastardization of 'ceirt') to apple trees with prayers or charms for the easing of trouble. As the rag rots, so goes the trouble.

It was popular to tie clooties on Beltane morning, and in fact the apple is intertwined with Beltane and Samhain: the two halves of the year, winter and spring. Times of change, times of uncertainty over the crop and the harvest. The apple blossoms in the spring and the ripe red apple of the fall link us with the same anxious hope: Let us get through this.

The apple is the tree that tells you, "Yes, times are going to be hard. And you're going to survive them." It will offer you the sustenance you need to get through hard times, as it's always offered mankind its bounty; the wonderful reds and russets of apple harvest are inextricably entwined with the winter closing in. "Here," the apple tree says, offering its lasting fruits, "take what I offer you, hard times are coming. Make sure you have sustenance for what's ahead." For the people of northern Europe, the apple was one of the staple winter foods. Packed with antioxidants, fiber, flavonoids and sugars, storing and lasting far longer than most ripe fruits, apples can help sustain animals and people when all other food has been exhausted. [2] Apples, like the tree they come from, are lasting.

Maybe this is why the apple tree is treated with such respect in the legends of Ireland. The people of ancient Ireland understood the value of this tree; in the Brehon laws, the Apple is listed as one of the Airig Fedo, Nobles of the Wood, and the punishment for harming one was quite a lot of wealth for the time period. In stories, the apple is a symbol of that which doesn't fade. In the tale of Echtrae Chonnlai [3] the apple has the power to regenerate itself and nourish him for a whole month:

Boí Connle íar sin co cenn mís cen dig cen biad, nabu fiu leis nach tóare do thomailt acht a ubull. Na nní do:meled, nícon:dígbad ní dend ubull acht ba hóg-som beos.

Thereafter, Connlae was without drink, without food until the end of a month, to him no sustenance was worth consuming save his apple.

And the isle to which King Arthur is brought wasn't originally called 'Avalon', it was *Avallach,* 'the land where there are apple trees'. [4] The apple trees took the king in their arms and, so the story goes, one day he'll come back all the stronger for it.

This is what the apple tells us: Hard times will come, and they will test us. We may bend under the strain. We may even break. But we will not die. After we've survived the storm, we'll grow again.

Speak

Blackberry

Trí fostadh:
foisdinecht,
gairde,
athchumairecht.

Three glories of speech: steadiness, wisdom, brevity.

Botanical name: *Rubus fruticosus*
Family: Rosaceae
Ogham: Muin
Scots Gaelic: Dris
Irish Gaelic: Sméar dubh
Welsh: Mwyar
French: La mûre

Message: Words have great power. You must use them wisely, but you must not fail to speak.

If you have been brambling or blackberrying in your life, you will soon understand the insight of linking this fid with the power of speech and the power of words. Brambles are not kind to the brash. In the *Aidedh Ferghusa meic Léide,* the king of the sidhe gives advice on species of trees, saying this about the bramble:

Bending wood the spiteful briar is,
burn he that is so keen and green;
He cuts, he flays the foot
the man that would rush forward he will hold back. [1]

But for those who are clever and careful, the blackberry yields its fruits.
Here we are given a perfect metaphor for the using of words.

Some have translated *muin* as 'grape vine', but archeological evidence calls that translation into question. According to Rowan Laurie, "grapevines are not native to Ireland and barely grow in its climate. They were a much later import and even in the warmest historical periods were difficult to cultivate." [2]

Although wine was imported from the Mediterranean as a high status drink as early as 600 BCE, [3] the plant from which it came was not part of the lore of old Ireland. The blackberry, on the other hand, appears again and again in poetry and song as the symbol of love, beauty and plenty. In the tales of Finn, a good summer is described as being 'of the beautiful blackberries', and in one of the most famous Irish love poems of all, the blackberry is used to denote beauty:

44

's í bláth deas na sú craobh í,	She's the blackberry-flower,
's í planda b'fhearr méin mhaith	the fine raspberry-flower,
le hamharc do shúl;	she's the plant of best breeding
's í mo chuisle, 's í mo rún í,	your eyes could behold;
's í bláth na n-úll gcumhra í,	she's my darling and dear,
is samhradh ins an fhuacht í	my fresh apple-tree flower,
idir Nollaig is Cáisc.	she is summer in the cold
	between Christmas and Easter. [4]

In the Brehon laws, the blackberry is marked as one of the 'sweet fruits' and a Bush of the Wood. Clearing a stand of them earned the penalty fee of a heifer cow. [5] The price was so high because these plants were so valuable as a food source. Rich in folates, potassium, vitamin E and sugars, they were a welcome supplement to the diet of ancient peoples. Blackberry seeds have been found in the remains of Neolithic man's stomach, blackberry shoots provided some of the first greens of spring, and ripe blackberries were an integral part of the Lughnasadh fairs, and the dishes served by lords to their client farmers and craftsmen at these times. [6] On the holy days, the usual system of clients paying their lords what they called 'food rent' was reversed, and lords held great *fled* or 'hospitality feasts' for their parishioners. The generosity of a lord was integral to his legitimacy: A lord who served bad fare could lose his holdings.

Why?

Because people talked. Unlike ancient England, which mainly focused on lineage as the deciding factor for one's place in the world, ancient Ireland was a contractual country. A free man signed a contract to be, say, a herdsman or a warrior with a specific lord, and his contract stipulated what he was owed in return for his service. If he liked the work and the terms, he renewed his contract on a yearly basis at the festival of Samhain. [7] If he did not, he found a new lord.

This created a system that placed great importance in the way an individual was spoken of and prized truthful speech. Again and again in period texts, liars are shamed and abused. In the Brehon law defamation of character incurred the same debt to the wounded party as a physical injury requiring two days of bed rest (8), and we have numerous historical examples of the price actually being demanded of someone who spoke falsely by a *brehon,* 'judge'. [9]

In this world, words truly had power. In this system, lords who were known to be stingy had fewer workers to tend their fields and beasts, fewer men to serve them under arms, and tended to suffer over time. A good master had good men. Thus, it paid to earn a reputation as a good lord and a good man. The man who did not remember this paid dearly for it.

One of the most famous stories in Ireland tells us just how high that price could be. It is the story of Caibre Mac Edaine the bard and Bres mac Eladain, who was high king.

In a world where words had power and the way others spoke of you decided your future, those who used words had enormous power. The Irish fillid went through intensive training to become walking libraries, able to advise on the past and record present events in ways that would make them easily remembered for the future. This recording included the great deeds of nobles, and the evil ones. Fillid were some of the first political satirists, and satire had a very practical purpose: To compose a satire against someone was to challenge their authority and call their honor into question. It was a potent weapon in an oral society.

The word *fillid* comes from the root word for 'sight', and Irish high bards were prized for their insight into situations and their clear articulation of history and present events. [10] By the time the *Uraichech Becc* law tract was written, the fili were of a higher social status than the druids and were classed with the lords, while the druids were classed as craftsmen. [11]

With this in mind, we can more easily understand the great crime Bres Mac Eladain did and why he paid for it.

Bres had proved himself an unpopular and thoughtless king when he took the throne after wounded Nuada was forced to abdicate. The boy was beautiful, but he had disdain for all under his rule. Forcing champions to carry firewood and lords to dig ditches, he humiliated them all from his high throne.

Now there came a cold night, and in it Caibre came knocking on the door of the king at Tara. "Lord I come to tell tales for my food and for my keep," he said when brought before Bres. The young king's lip curled. "Well then, be about it," he said.

And so Caibre sang and spoke the evening away for Bres and his folk. But when he had done his work he was taken, not to a good pallet in the castle, but to an outer shed.

It was narrow, dark, and dim. There was neither fire, nor bath, nor bed. Three small oat cakes were brought to him for dinner. Neither butter nor milk was offered. Caibre slept cold and hungry that night.

In the morning, he stood before the court and spoke. "Lord, I have a poem on your hospitality."

"Well, be about it." said Bres.

And Caibre spoke.

"Without food upon the platter,
Without a cow's milk whereon calf thrives,
Without a house in the deep darkness,
Be that the luck of Bres Mac Eladain."

The bard swept away in a flap of cloak. "Bres's wealth will fail," he said as he passed the threshold.

And as the bard said, it was so. By nightfall, Bres had broken out in hives, and by Samhain he had lost the contracts of his men. Soon he lost the throne.

The words we speak have great power for good and ill. We must remember to use our words in ways that help the folk and the world around us. Speak to raise another's spirits. Speak to right a wrong. Speak to heal what's harmed. Be thoughtful when you raise your voice, always. But never be afraid.

Grow

Ivy

Moaighthe:
médaighthe, sochair,
do neoch.

Three sounds of increase:
the lowing of a cow in milk,
the din of a smithy,
the swish of a plough.
-From *The Triads of Ireland*

Botanical name: *Hedera helix*
Family: Araliaceae
Ogham: Gort
Scots Gaelic: Eidheann
Irish Gaelic: Eidhneán
Welsh: Eiddew
French: Lierre

Message: It is time to plant seeds and start ventures. Reach up, reach out, and grow.

The word for this fid in the Ogham translates as 'greenest of pastures' or 'sweetest of grass'. Picture a green pasture under a spring sky, cattle grazing placidly in the grass with full udders. To the passerby, nothing is quite so idyllic.

But the passerby does not see the hours of work the landowner puts in to spread muck and bone meal over the pasture in order to fertilize it. The passerby does not see the quiet, patient hours the farmer puts in with a cow in labor, waiting to help her birth her calf. The beauty of a perfect garden and a well-tended field is made possible only through the sweat of the farmer and the hand of the gardener. This is the fid of that work and its reward. The ivy thrives because it is tenacious, and it is resilient.

The plant itself is not a good food for humans: all parts of the plant, particularly the berries, are filled with the saponins didehydrofalcarinol, falcarinol and hederasaponin. [1] These chemicals can cause intestinal and breathing issues in humans if ingested in large quantities. Cattle, on the other hand, can benefit from small doses of ivy, especially as a supplement in the days when winter fodder was not purchased but grown. In Fergus Kelly's work, *Early Irish Farming*, it's noted that through the 7th and 8th centuries, harvesting ivy to feed the kine in winter was so common that a specific tool, the *cromán tige bantrebthaige*, 'hook of a woman householder', was recorded in law tracts. [2] The plant was valued highly enough to be recorded as one of the 'bushes of the wood' in the Brehon law, and clearing a tract of it unlawfully earned the offender the fine of a year old heifer. [3]

The sense of this comes clear with the knowledge that, in the climate of the British Isles, ivy is one of the brightest of evergreens in the depths of winter, and its utility in feeding the animals the Irish based their system of status on was enormously important. Its symbolism of sustained fertility in adversity is bound into winter festivities, and depending on who you ask, it stands for many things related to hope in the darkness. In England, the ivy king and the holly king vie on Yule or on New Year's Day, ivy standing for summer and the green time of year. As he lost in the autumn, now he has the strength to win and bring summer back. [4] In Ireland, it was the oak king and not the ivy who won, but the ivy and the holly together stood for everlasting life. [5] We still see this in the song "The Holly and the Ivy", as in these verses:

The holly and the ivy,
When they are both full grown
Of all the trees that are in the wood
The holly bears the crown!

O the rising of the sun
And the running of the deer
The playing of the merry organ
Sweet singing of the choir [6]

Throughout Ireland, male holly and the female ivy tied together in wreaths and charms were hung to keep the people hoping in the dark days. Of course, this being the Isles, at times these traditions blend, and we see some songs where ivy is a queen denied entry or power while holly rules the winter, as in "Nay Ivy Nay", a song from the age of Henry VIII:

Nay, Ivy, nay, it shall not be, I wis,
Let Holly have the mastery as the manner is!

Holly standeth in the hall fair to behold,
Ivy stands without the door; she is full sore an' cold! [7]

In some areas, one of the winter games was a tug of war between holly boys and ivy girls, one more symbol of the fight to survive the winter and bring in the summer heat. [8]

After winter, ivy was a symbol of cultivation and industry in both the positive and negative. Ivy was used as a symbol of tenacity and fertility, but it's also a pest. Armed with adventitious roots and an amazing growth ability, in wet areas ivy can spread frighteningly fast. Once it gets its hooked rootlets into tree bark, it can grow upwards to 50-100' in height. On the ground, it typically grows to 6-9" tall but spreads over time to 50-100'. [9] It can dig the mortar out of stone buildings and kill trees that it colonizes through blocking of their light and damaging of their bark. At times throughout the history of Ireland, men have fought ivy to keep pastures open and allow more nutritious plants to grow: grasses for the cattle, barley for the people. Controlling ivy was one of the necessary chores of cultivation, and not one of the easiest.

Controlling wild growth and channeling the energy into useful purposes was, and still is, the main work of those embarking on tasks intended to bring forth a harvest. The task of cultivation demands three things: discipline, patience, and tenacity. As it is today, so it was in the beginning of things, when people first began to work the land.

The *Lebor Gabála Érenn*, the 'Book of the Takings of Ireland', tells us how it was for the first people who worked and tended the soil.

The tale is told to us through Fintan, one of the first people to arrive in Ireland. Unable to do the duty of working the land himself with his own people under Queen Cesair, Fintan hid himself away and became the recorder of all the folk who came after, living in the forms of animals to extend his life and his knowledge of the land.

In the form of an eagle, he watched Cesair's fifty women die out, for he and the two men she had brought had all failed in their duties to bring about a second generation. He sings:

> I was here in Ireland
> and Ireland was desert
> Ireland was waste,
> for a space of three hundred years,
> till Partholon came to it

Parthalon's people set to work on the great barren plain. Fintan tells us in his poetry:

> Four chieftains strong came with Partholon:
> himself and Laiglinne his son, from whom is Loch Laighlinne
> Slanga and Rudraige, the two other sons of Partholon,
> from whom are Sliab Slanga and Loch Rudraige
> When they began their digging,
> the lake there burst forth over the land.

There were seven lake bursts in Ireland in the time of Partholon
Four plains were cleared by Partholon in Ireland
For Partholon found not more than one plain in Ireland before him

Through the lifetimes of Eagle and Stag, Boar and finally Salmon, Fintan watched as each people put their hands and their lives into the soil of the land. The Parthalonians died by plague and their bodies grew rich grass. The Nemedians came to plant the great forests of Ireland. They defended the land against the destruction of those who did not care to till and cultivate, but came to loot and kill. When their time passed and Fintan was a boar, the Fir Bolg built Ireland's hills so that the rain would run to feed the land. The Tuatha De Dannan planted the great bile trees and partitioned the country into its five provinces, fighting the forces of destruction all the while. At last, when the Milesians from whom the Irish people descended set foot upon the land, it was a rich and fertile place. A lady caught a salmon, ate it, and nine months later a boy was born who told the tale of all the ages that had come before.

It would have been easy for any one of the seven races to throw up their hands, get in their boats and go elsewhere. It would have been easy to simply accept what was there. But each generation worked the land, cultivated it and helped it grow into its full glory. That is the virtue of the ivy: persistent, tenacious hope. Ivy will tell you that all the work is worth your while, and every failure is merely a step towards something greater.

What you tend will flourish and bear fruit. But you must be there to tend it.

Heal

Broom

Tréde neimthigedar liaig:
Dígallrae,
díainme,
comchissi cen ainchiss

Three things that constitute a
physician:
a complete cure,
The leaving of no blemish,
a painless examination
-From *The Triads Of Ireland*

Botanical name: *Cytisus scoparius*
Family: Fabaceae
Ogham: Ngeatal
Scots Gaelic: Bealaidh
Irish Gaelic: Giolcach shléibhe
Welsh: Banadl gorweddol
French: Balai

Message: In making yourself whole, you aid in the healing of those around you. In making others whole,
you aid in the healing of the world.

There are times in northern Europe when the skies are gray for days. It seems the sun will never return.
You are trudging along a muddy lane, your spirits at lowest ebb . . . and then you raise your eyes. In the
grayness, there is a speck of sunfire. It is the flowering broom, bright as a candle flame.

This bushy plant has many names in the Isles: bizzom, broom, and whin are the most common, and it is
confused with gorse often in passing. [1] Evergreen and ever-blooming, it was once believed, the plant
was one of the most popular wedding and celebration decorations well into the 20th century. [2] Broom
was carried at weddings for its luck, burned as a torch to promote health, fed young to cattle, people and
sheep in winter to provide missing vitamins in the diet [3] and brewed into a heady mead. [4] At Eastertide
it was common to form flowering broom into besoms and clean the house out for the year, and scrubbing
pads for floors and walls were often made from the wire-like branches. The plant was a favorite for
thatching houses as well. [5] But the hand that would pluck the broom must do so with care, for the long,
whippy branches are lined with corded bark inlaid with silica, and a grasping hand will be sliced, every
wound embedded with splinters of bark. [6] As the plant can both cause and treat deep wounds, the Irish
word for the fid refers to both the wound and the healer who will cure it. When we carelessly harvest
broom, as when we do so many things carelessly, we learn a painful lesson. Broom's tough bark can, and
will, lacerate our flesh. If we ignore the wounds, they will fester. The longer a splinter is left in the flesh,
the greater the pain and the sickness it causes will grow. Ignoring a wound may seem less painful than
seeking the cause of it, but in the end the wounds that we do not treat are the ones that will ruin us. Yet
we persist and work in spite of the injury. Why?

Sometimes we think we have no choice. Sometimes we fear the ridicule of others when they see our
wound and mock us for our weakness. But the man who sits down, cleans the blood and splinters from

his hands and returns to work better than he was does not show weakness. He shows wisdom. And the man who mocks another for his injuries shows not his own strength, but his own stupidity. Injury and illness do not affect the worth of the afflicted individual. Again and again, the old texts make this point. Cormac Mac Art wrote:

Do not mock the elderly, though you be young;
Nor the poor, though you be rich;
Nor the ragged, though you be wealthy;
Nor the lame, though you be fleet.
Nor the blind, though you can see;
Nor the weak, though you be strong;
Nor the senseless, though you be prudent;
Nor the foolish though you be wise. [7]

And in *The Triads of Ireland* we read:

Trí buirb in betha:	Three rude ones of the world:
óc contibi sen,	a youngster mocking an old man,
slán contibi galarach,	a healthy person mocking an invalid,
gáeth contibi báeth.	a wise man mocking a fool [8]

Again and again, we see the theme. The old man who is mocked is in fact the powerful mage of the story, the old woman who is insulted on the road is one of the *sidhe*. Equating the worth of a person with their affliction is a grave error of the one making the judgement, whether that judgement concerns oneself or another. You will never know when a shoddy exterior might hide great worth.

In a niche overlooking the king's baths at Bath, England, there sits a regal figure. The inscription below reads 'Bladud, son of Lud Hudibrus, Eight King of the Britons, founder of these baths'.

It is the story of the founding that will teach us.

As a young man, Bladud (pronounced 'bla-dith') was the treasure of his family and his people. A brilliant scholar, Bladud was sent to Greece for eleven years of study. On the day he was due to return, his royal parents prepared the court for a fete.

But it was not a brave young man who rode through the gates: it was a wretched boy, covered in sores. The queen cried out.

"My son, what ails you?"

Bladud whispered a word that shook his parents to the core:

"Leprosy."

At the word, the subjects of the court cried out in panic, demanding the banishment of the pestilence. Bladud turned away without a word. But his mother cried his name, and cast her ring into the dirt at his feet.

53

"If the gods heal you, this ring will prove you are my beloved boy."

Bladud kept the ring against his heart as he left his home once more, stripped of his title and his pride. He wandered for a year and a day, driven out of every place, until he came to the great oak forests of the River Avon. There a swineherd saw him wandering.

"Man, a bed and your meals for your eyes on my pigs, what say you?"

"I say aye," Bladud replied gratefully.

From that day he watched over the pigs under the oak trees, feeding them on rich acorn crops. He might have lived like this for all his life. But one winter's evening, he camped beneath Solsbury Hill with his pigs. And in the morning, the pigs were gone.

Bladud searched in a panic, finding the tracks of his pigs and trailing them to a place where they were rolling joyfully in mud. Bracing himself for the cold slime, Bladud stepped in.

To his shock, the mud was warm.

One by one and two by two, he wrangled and tempted his pigs out of the mud and into the River Avon for a wash. To his amazement, every scratch and scar that forest living had given his pigs were washed away with the mud, as were his leprous wounds and ruined flesh.

Laughing and giving his thanks, he drove his charges back to their owner, and turned his feet towards home.

"Who are you?" the guards at the gate of his home demanded, for they saw a farm man only. Bladud held up his mother's ring.

"I am the king that will be."

Returned to his health and his place, the first thing Bladud did was bestow the lands and the lordship of a town upon the swineherd who offered him a place when the world shunned him. The town is still known as Hogs Norton. That done, Bladud set about building a shrine around the hot springs he'd found, in his pious thanks for the healing he was given. That place of healing still stands today.

The broom's branches are dangerous, but its flowers are bright.

"I know it hurts," broom murmurs, "but it will be worth the pain to become greater than you were yesterday. This is how you heal. This is how you become more than you are today."

Change

Blackthorn

Am gáeth tar na bhfarraige
Am tuile os chinn maighe
Am dord na daíthbhe
Am damh seacht mbeann
Am drúchtín rotuí ó ngréin
Am an fráich torc
Am seabhac a néad i n-aill
Am ard filidheachta
Am álaine bhláithibh
Am an t-eo fis
Cía an crann agus an theine ag tuitim faire?

I am a wind across the sea
I am a flood across the plain
I am the roar of the tides
I am a stag of seven tines
I am dew in the sun
I am the wildest of boars
I am a hawk on the cliff
I am a height of poets
I am the most beautiful among flowers
I am the salmon of wisdom
Who but I is both the tree and the lightning
striking it?
-From the *Book of the Takings Of Ireland*

Botanical name: *Prunus spinosa*
Family: Prunus
Ogham: Straif
Scots Gaelic: Àirneag,
Irish Gaelic: Draighean
Welsh: Draenen ddu
French: Prunelliers

At a height of 18 feet, blackthorn is not a tree of great stature, but its lore stands tall indeed. The blackthorn is the tree of transformation, changing all things it touches.

Blackthorn transforms landscapes. Across the British Isles, the blackthorn was planted in tight hedges. The qualities of its thorns, its thick wood and its tenacity even in salt-laden ground near the coasts made it the first choice when people created hedges that were impossible for domestic animals to assail. In the words of the Brehon law, a good blackthorn hedge should be pruned so that "a small pig should not be able to penetrate on account of its closeness, and an ox should not be able to penetrate on account of its height and firmness." [1] Not many creatures could endure the pain of a blackthorn's piercing branches, and thus blackthorn hedges divided the land into parcels throughout the isles.

Blackthorn marks the changes of the year. At the death of the old year, the advent of frost is told by the ripening fruits of blackthorn: its sloes are sweetened into edibility only by the first hard frosts of winter. Some say the handle of the Callieach Bheur's frost-hammer is blackthorn, and that when she hits the earth to freeze it over on Samhain night, it's the magic of blackthorn she uses. In Ulster the queen of winter needs no hammer, only a cudgel of blackthorn to blast the land into its winter barrenness. [2]

But as it marks the death of the year, blackthorn will mark its birth as well. It blooms white in the liminal month of March, when winter has not quite given up her grip. This relationship between the wariness agricultural people have for early spring and this plant is recorded in the English and Scottish nickname for spiteful late-spring storms: these blighting snowfalls are called 'blackthorn winter'. [3] The flowers are not trusty signs of summer, but they are signs of hope in the dark.

Blackthorn transforms cloth. Every part of the plant is used in the dyer's art: a green dye from the leaves, a grey dye from the sloes, a yellow dye from the bark boiled in alkali, an orange dye from the flowers boiled with alum, a deep red from the roots, a purple if iron was added. In old Ireland these colors meant much: Your clothing was your calling card. What has survived to come down to us of the Brehon laws came mostly from 30 manuscripts rescued by Edward Llwyd in the 1780s. [4] These papers are written in archaic forms of Old Irish and extremely difficult to discern at times, but what is agreed upon is something like this:

The unfree were allowed to wear three colors.

The low free man was allowed four colors in his dress.

The farmer and crofter was allowed four colors in his dress, brown and bright red included.

The craftsman was allowed four colors, blue, brown and red included.

The noble, the brehon and the scholar was allowed five colors.

The king of a kingdom of Ireland was allowed six colors.

The high king and the first of the orders of bards, brehons, and druids were allowed the wearing of seven colors at one time.

Even today, what we choose to wear has power, though the meanings are no longer so clearly defined. Change your clothes, change yourself in the perceptions of those around you. If you are aware of this, it can be used as a great power.

And then there were those times when blackthorn changed people. Sometimes it turned them into braver people. Other times, it turned them into corpses.

If you cut a stout stave of blackthorn near the bole of the plant, you'll end up with a heavy stick that has a knob near the end. Strip this of bark, rub it with butter or lanolin and let it cure in a chimney over the winter. Take it out and what you will have is a stout, shining shillelagh: just long enough to be a walking stick, just heavy enough to be a formidable weapon. [5] A young man travelling for the first time was often gifted a shillelagh for his defense on the road: holding a stout weapon he could rely on and trained in its use, he need have no fear. The Irish martial art of bataireacht, the traditional fighting style using the shillelagh, focused on knocking the opponent to their knees or laying them on their backs, where tradition dictated they ought to yield. This allowed for formal and honorable single combat without death to exist as a last resort for settling disputes or cooling hot tempers. [6] As time went by and outsiders did not honor custom, the shillelagh became a more fearsome weapon. In the west around the 17th century, a terrifying habit grew up of shaping the blackthorn with a single remaining thorn, designed to cause puncture wounds on impact that would fester and kill the victim. The heads of shillelagh were filled with lead to create fearsome skull-crushers. In days when the Irish knew they were travelling to unfriendly lands, they made sure to carry their shillelagh so much so that it became associated with Irish identity for centuries afterwards. [7] Even a small person could feel confident with a shillelagh in their hands, and even a well-built bully would reconsider when they spotted one in the hands of their prey.

Some changes look like loss and some like gain, but they are two facets of one truth: we must change in order for our own growth and for the growth of our world. The theme of a change that appears as a death and is only a new way of being appears again and again in the lore of Wales, England, Ireland and Scotland. But among its many masters, none is quite so great as Taliesin.

In days past, the lady Cerridwen had a son named Afaggdu who was as ugly as he was stupid. His name meant 'utter darkness'. Like any good mother, the lady wished better for her son.

In her cauldron, she collected all the herbs and ingredients she would need. This working was to be so great that the person who first tasted of it would be gifted with all the knowledge in the world.

So the cauldron simmered for a year and a day. Cerridwen put an old blind man to work feeding the fire, and a young servant boy named Gwion stirring the brew.

On the last day of the spell, a bubble in the cauldron burst, sending a few scalding drops onto Gwion's finger. The boy cried out in pain and instinctively put his finger into his mouth to cool it. At that instant, Gwion gained the knowledge that was meant for Afaggdu.

Enraged, Cerridwen took off after the boy. "I'll have your life!" she screamed.

Gwion was in great terror. But he was in great power as well, possessed of all knowledge. So the boy turned himself into a hare and ran into the blackthorn to escape Cerridwen. The lady became a hunting hound and burrowed after.

Gwion came to a stream and changed himself into a quick-swimming trout, but Cerridwen was an otter, fast behind him. The trout leaped from the water and became a swift sparrow, but Cerridwen was a hawk.

Just as her talons were outstretched to catch, Gwion spied a wheat field, and so he turned into a grain of wheat. Cerridwen became a hen and gobbled him up. And so, she thought, that was the end of the boy Gwion.

Not long after, Cerridwen found herself with child. For nine months she carried the babe she knew to be Gwion. Cerridwen intended to kill the child as soon as it was born, In the fullness of time she gave birth to a grand boy, and her plans were foiled by the thing she hadn't expected: love for a child come of her womb.

But Afaggdu had not forgotten that this child had stolen the knowledge meant for him. Cerridwen knew of his hate: her second son would never live long in Afaggdu's presence. So the lady crafted a tiny boat and set her second son adrift in the sea.

The babe came to rest on the shores of what we know today as Wales. The craft was found by a man named Elphin, nephew of Maelgwyn, king of Dyfed. Resolved to foster the child as his own son, Elphin named the boy Taliesin, which means 'shining brow'.

So came into the world Taliesin, changed many times over and the greater for it.

Do not fear change, even when it comes wearing the mask of death. A seed that never ends its present existence will never grow.

Feel

Elder

Tréde neimthigedar cruitire:
golltraige, gentraige, súantraige.

Three things that constitute a harper: a
tune to make you cry, a tune to make you
laugh, a tune to give you peace.
-From *The Triads of Ireland*

Botanical name: *Sambucus nigra*
Family: Adoxaceae
Ogham: Ruis
Scots Gaelic: Droman
Irish Gaelic: Trom
Welsh: Ysgawen
French: Sureau

Message: Your emotions are the lords in the hall of your soul, but you are the ruler. Be counseled by
your passions, but do not let them rule you.

Ruis translates directly as 'the red of passion' or 'the red of emotion'. But there are many ways to be red
with emotion:

Crimson with rage.
Red in the face with laughter.
Blushing in shame.
Red-eyed with weeping.

So it is with the elder tree. It is a plant of complex meanings. White-flowered in late spring and sweet-
berried in late autumn, it is both a food and a poison. Its leaves contain cyanogenic glycosides [1] and can
kill, but its flowers and berries are lauded in the form of elderflower wine, elderberry cordial, jams,
roasted fritters, and all manner of pastries and delicacies. Neither black nor white, evil nor good in
whole, the elder tree grows in sheltered, damp places, bent over herself as if protecting secrets. She is a
plant of nuances and twilight places.

Elder is the tree of the musician. Paul Kendall writes in *Trees for Life*, "Wood from the elder tree lends
itself well to the making of whistles, pipes, chanters and other musical instruments, as the branches
contain a soft pithy core which is easily removed to create hollow pipes of a pale, hard, easily-polished
wood." [2] In a time before our entertainments, the talented musician was a prize among folk. We can still
see it in the names people wear: in *A History of Irish Music,* William Flood tells us, "The CURTIN
(MacCurtin) family is so named from a hereditary skill on the cruit; whilst the family names TUMPANE
and TUMPANY are derived from a musical ancestry–famous timpanists, or performers on the timpan.
The music of this latter instrument was generally known as a dump; and various dumps are to be met

with in MS. music books of the 16th century. A similar musical origin is traced for the surnames Harper, Piper, Fiddler, etc., whilst the family of MACCROSSAN (now Englished CROSBIE) are so-called from the Irish word Crossan–a travelling musical comedian. The CRONINS or CRONANS are in like manner designated from a family of street singers. Similarly, the family name Mac an Bhaird, or Ward, which really means "son of the bard," is derivable from a bardic origin." [3]

Music was the lifeblood of the folk. It lent joy to a long day. It led the charge for battle. Music was played at a birth, a marriage and a death. Music was the teaching tool the bards and brehons used to imprint their lessons on their listeners. Among the learned music was what was described as the Three Noble Strains:

The *Goiltrai* or 'sorrow strain' allowed people to weep.
The *Geantrai* or 'joy strain' encouraged people to laugh.
The *Suantrai* or 'sleep strain' gave people peace and helped them sleep.

It's telling that the suffix of these words, *trai*, translates as 'magic'. On flutes and pipes of elder wood, on drums with elder wood bodies, on harps with oaken sound boxes and elder wood inlays every emotion was played: the music of pain and the music of joy, the music of weeping and the music of the battlefield. We cannot live as whole people without hearing each of these musics. Every note has its place, every emotion its purpose. The art of the musician is to weave them into a harmony, no single sound drowning out the others. That is how music is made.

Learning music, like learning to balance emotions within ourselves, requires intense study and regular practice. But it is worth the work. In the days of the Brehon law, a person–man or woman–who attained mastery of the harp raised their honor price to that of a noble, and their harp was given the worth of a human life. [4] In the literature of Old Ireland, we read again and again warnings against intemperate or uncontrolled emotional outbursts. Fury in the battlefield might be valued, but fury in the home or the hall was a crime. The bard Caibre asked the scholar-king Cormac Mac Art once:

"O grandson of Conn, Cormac, what is best for a king?'
'Not hard to tell,' said Cormac. 'Best for him:
Composure rather than wrath,
Patience without strife,
Affability rather than arrogance' [4]

In *The Triads* of Ireland we read warnings again and again to keep ourselves in balance:
Tréde conaittig fírinne: mess, tomus, cubus.
Three things which justice demands: judgment, measure, conscience.

Trí cuitbidi in domain: fer lonn, fer étaid, fer díbech.
Three laughing-stocks of the world: an angry man, a jealous man, a miser.

In modern Irish, this tradition has continued in slightly more oblique and humorous terms:
Is minic a bhris béal duine a shrón.
Many a time a man's mouth broke his nose. [5]

All people were expected to have their emotions, even to show them. But woe betide the one who let those emotions rule them: losing your temper had a high cost. There were penalties in the Brehon laws for unlawfully satirizing, 'harming the honor' (we would call it embarrassing) or humiliating another person as well as there were laws for causing physical harm when you were in a temper. One Brehon's record remarks in the margin:

Trí comartha clúanaigi: búaidriud scél, cluiche tenn, abucht co n-imdergad.
Three ungentlemanly things: interrupting stories, a mischievous game, jesting so as to raise a blush. [6]

With your words you could take something precious away from others: their pride and their confidence. The ancient Irish recognized this in law. In penance, you would pay a physical fee, but you also paid a social price: your community had seen you act like a lout, and your entire community saw the shame written on your face.

When we are ashamed or emotionally overwrought, our body shows it clearly: we blush. This is especially obvious in the people who had lost most of the melanin in their skin to survive in the climates of the British Isles. The blush of shame, red as the name of this fid, is one of the most frustrating parts of life even in our modern world. I imagine many of us wish fervently that we didn't have this biological mechanism. Little as we may appreciate it, this uncontrollable reaction serves an important function in human society: our bodies are showing with glaring clarity that we know something is wrong in the social situation. We are, essentially, showing that we have social awareness and are affected by the reactions of those around us. This is the most essential trait social creatures possess. It's what allows us to continue to cohabit in relative harmony. And it may have a hidden benefit for the individual as well.

In an article for *The Psychologist*, Ray Crozier writes of blushing in these words: "It signals the blusher's adherence to society's rules, norms and standards and acknowledgement of failure to comply with them. This can deflect any hostile reaction from others, help the group to strengthen its bond and avoid spending resources on aggressive acts. Psychological research has considered that a blush communicates appeasement, a non-verbal apology or has a remedial function, helping to put matters right after some social predicament (Edelmann, 2001).

"Empirical studies find that people who blush when they have violated some norm are viewed less negatively than people who don't blush in these circumstances." [7]

As much as you may want to sink into the floor when your shame is written on your face, you must understand that your shame is not your enemy. You are contributing to the subtle social fabric that holds us all together. If we felt no shame at all, we would not survive.

Any emotion can become warped as it grows. Any emotion can sicken inside us and become harmful. But if we take the time to pay attention to our emotions, recognize and understand them, they become powerful tools.

In the days when the Tuatha De Dannan still fought for the soul and soil of Ireland, emotions served to win a battle and right a wrong.

It's said that the Dagda, eldest and earthiest of the Tuatha, was a great harper. He was the proud holder of the harp Uaithne, She of the Four Angled Music. Made from oak and inlaid with elder wood, she was a lovely thing. He took her with him to the battlefield during the Second Battle of Mag Tuired, using her to raise the spirits of his folk on the night before the battle where they hoped to overthrow the tormentors who had harried them for three decades.

After the victorious battle and the routing of his enemies, the Dagda found his harp missing. In an act of spite, the Formorians had taken it as they fled.

Realizing what had been done, the Dagda called his son Aengus Og to him. "Come now lad. We're off to fetch my four angled beauty."

Carefully, they tracked their foes to the Formorian camp at a fort. Inside Bres, Formorian king, criminal and traitor, was at table with his lords. Grumbling, they sat together and licked their wounds. Through a chink in the door, father and son could just make out the candle flames outlining the harp, hanging on the wall over Bres's head. Seeing it, the Dagda began to chant:

Come *Daurdabla*, apple-sweet murmurer
Come, *Coir-cethair-chuir*, four-angled frame of harmony,
Come summer, come winter,
Out of the mouths of harps and bags and pipes!

The harp on the wall slid from her bonds and flew to his hands, breaking the doors asunder. Some say she left nine warriors dead in her wake.

Before the moment of shocked silence at such a thing was over, the Dagda began to play.

He played the weeping strain of the *goltrai*, and the Formorians mourned their defeat.

Then he played the joyful strain of the *geantrai*, and the Formorians fell about in drunken laughter.

Finally, he played the sleeping strain of the *suantrai*, and the Formorians lay themselves down and slept all through the camp, the pains of battle eased.

Heads held high, the Dagda and his son walked out of the encampment with Uaithne.

The elder offers you her wood and her wisdom. Cut a branch with care, make yourself an instrument. The notes are your emotions. Understood, they make a music. Out of place, they make discordant racket.

The choice of what you make is yours.

Build

Pine

Teora ranna sluinte fri cáintocad:
trumma,
toicthiu,
talchaire

Your good fortune has three parts:
Your surety
Your discipline
Your will
-From the *Book of Ballymote*

Botanical name: *Pinus sylvestris*
Family: Pinaceae
Ogham: Ailm
Scots Gaelic: Guibhas
Irish Gaelic: Giúis
Welsh: Pinwydden
French: Pin

Message: It is time to put in the hard work of honing your craft and cultivating your work.

In the rocky slopes of Northern Ireland, the pines creak in the wind. When one falls or is felled, there is a long, high keening as pliant timbers resist the breaking and the fall. This is perhaps why one of the tracts for this fid in the Ogham names it *ardam íachta,* 'loudest of cries'. [1]

But the felling of a pine tree is only the very first step towards the making of something new.

The Scots pine is native from Scandinavia to Anatolia, growing where the land is poor: rocky outcrops, peat bogs, the very edges of forested land. [2] On fertile ground, it is crowded out by others. Where other trees wither, it thrives. A symbol of tenacity, its branches were cut and hung throughout halls and houses at the winter celebrations, mixed into holly and ivy to mark the folk's defiance of darkness and despair. Mixing these three creates a potent charm for those who know the Ogham: while the holly lends the fire of inspiration and the ivy gives its vitality, it is pine that gives the bearer the will to carry on the work. The only native conifer to the British Isles, the Scots pine was the greatest reminder the Irish people had that the green world was sleeping in winter, not dead. [3]

The wood of the Scots pine was the most versatile of all trees. While not as hard as oak nor as pliant as willow, it was tough, light, easily worked and resistant to decay. [4] Stands of pine were quick to grow back when cut. This made it a favorite wood for daily work. Pine wood was turned to all manner of daily things: wheels and wooden spoons, fences and pit props, gate posts and firewood. Its heartwood was used in the building of ships, and its sap in the caulking of them. [5] For its uses it was named in the Brehon laws as one of the Nobles of the Wood, described as 'friend to the joiner' and 'hand of the carpenter' in the Auraicept na n-eces. [6]

In the past, the work of carpentry covered every step from selecting the proper tree to putting the final polish on the finished work. The work is neither quick nor easy.

The tree must be selected and cut.

The log must be limbed and sawn to the desired thickness.

The sawn wood must be stacked, or it will stain.

The wood must be aged carefully over the span of a year.

The wood must be well measured, cut, and carefully worked.

The finish work must be rubbed with beeswax or lanolin. [7]

The process is long, and things can go wrong at any step. A tree that seems healthy can prove to be rotten in the center and worthless. Wood warps, splits, and cracks in drying. Wood splits when being worked, rendering the work unusable. [8]

The impatient student of carpentry will soon give up in despair.

But pine is the first wood a carpenter is allowed to work with. Pine teaches perseverance. In the working of pine wood, the student learns tenacity.

The student should learn, as well, the difference between a flaw in their work and a flaw of their character. Every student will fail. Every carpenter will toss away pieces of his work, accepting that the time spent in the rejects was spent in learning. It was not wasted. The worthwhile student is the one who raises their head, lifts their tools and starts again, remembering what they've learned. That is how he becomes a craftsman.

Once, it was a man's tenacity that saved a people.
Long and long ago, Finn MacCool, warrior-magician who would one day be a great leader of men, was out riding when he noticed men working away at a hill fort. He was still a very young man and, being curious, reigned in his horse.

"When will the rath be finished?" he asked politely. One of the men gave a rueful laugh.

"Probably never."

"Why?" asked Finn.

"Every day we raise this rath, but each night it is burnt to the ground. Whatever we do, we sleep in the night, and when we wake the rath is burnt. We may leave soon and choose a new place."
Curious, Finn bit his thumb in which his gift of knowledge was held, and discovered the secret of what had been happening. Soon, night would fall.

"If you'll let me stand guard tonight, I will find the trouble."

Finn had learned from the secret knowledge he was gifted with that on the eastern side of the country, there lived an old hag with three sons. She hated the king, and every evening at nightfall she sent the youngest to spell the men to sleep and burn the king's rath. So he waited. Now night was coming on, and the old woman in the east told her youngest son to hurry on with his torches.

Soon the warriors began to doze, all save Finn and his dog Bran. Soon there was a speeding ball of fire. The hag's son threw the torches upon the thatched roof to set it alight. But Finn's dog Bran was quick and tossed the torches into the stream.

"Who is this," cried the youngest son of the old hag, "who has dared to put out my lights?"

"I," said Fin. The hag's son lashed out. Bran came down from the rath to help Fin: she bit and tore his enemy's back while Finn fought him. When he turned to fight the dog, Finn ran him through.

In the east the hag said "You take torches and hurry on, see why your brother is slow."

Soon a second ball of fire came streaking across the sky, and Finn slew the second son of the hag.

The old woman was raging at the delay in the east. "Now take torches," she snapped to her eldest and strongest son, "go and see what delays your brothers; I'll pay them for this when they come home."

The eldest brother shot off through the air, came to the king's rath, and threw his torches upon the roof. They had just singed the straw a little when Bran pushed them off.

"Who is this," screamed the eldest, "who dares to interfere?"

"I," shouted Fin. And the third son fought and died.

Finn thought he could rest now. But once again, flame shot across the sky. The old hag herself had come, far more terrible than any of her sons.

The battle was long and bloody. Just as daylight was coming, Fin lopped the head off the old woman.

"You are the man who saved the rath," said the king of the land, "and yours is the reward. Would you become my battle chieftain and lead my men?"

"That I will," said Finn. And that was the first time Finn led men.

The scent of pine woods and cut pine raises the spirit. It clears the head. Take a breath and remember that there is honor in hard work. There is no shame in failure. The only shame is in surrender: in giving into despair and turning from the work.

Do not turn away.

Move

Gorse

a good season is summer for long journeys:
quiet is the tall fine wood which the wind will
not stir
green is the plumage of the sheltering wood
eddies swirl in the stream
good is the warmth in the turf.
-From *The Book of Invasions*

Botanical name: *Ulex europaeus*
Family: Fabaceae
Ogham: Onn
Scots Gaelic: Conasg
Irish Gaelic: Aiteann gallda
Welsh: Heithin
French: Ajoncs

Message: It's time to move, to travel, to see new things and to see things in new ways.

The word of this fid, O*nn*, translates as 'wheel'. From the same root word as the sole of the foot in Old Irish, the gorse plant lines the roads in gold, tempting you to follow and see where it leads.

An evergreen shrub standing 7 to 10 feet tall, this plant was a favorite for roadside hedges throughout Britain and Ireland for two reasons: it acted as a road marker and an impenetrable barrier. When weather turned misty or foul in Ireland, many a traveler was kept on the road and out of bogs by the lines of bright yellow blooms to either side of the track. Gorse blooms reliably from December through the following November, making it a natural road marker. [1] And if the wanderer didn't see the plant, he'd certainly feel it should he bump into one of the hedge bushes. Gorse has thorns as long as a grown man's little finger, and they are not much tampered with by humans.

We may leave it alone, but grazing animals love the taste of gorse. It is listed in the Brehon laws as one of the 'bushes of the wood', and as such, stands of the bush were open to as much cutting or work as a farmer might choose to do on them. [2] This made it accessible for many farming-adjacent uses, and to many uses was it put.

First and foremost, it was used to feed horses. In the word-Ogham associated with each fid in the *Auraicept na n-Éces*, the fid of *Onn* is described many times as 'the helper of horses' or 'beloved of horses.' This makes a great deal of sense with a little botanical knowledge: Gorse is in the same plant family as peas, beans and clovers, gorse fixes nitrogen due to symbiosis with a bacterium in the roots. This makes it a valuable plant for the soil and the animals that browse on it, rich with protein, nitrogen and trace elements. [3] It was an integral part of the diet for horses and cows in Old Ireland especially, where gorse was such an important crop it was specifically registered in legal documents in the 15th and 16th centuries as an asset on farm land. [4]

It's written in *Farming in Ireland* that "20 statute acres of gorse should support 100 head of cattle for the winter six months without other food save the morning feed of mangold wurzel turnips or potatoes.

"The saving of hay for 100 cows would be at least £200 per annum, enabling the small farmer to feed eight milch cows off the same space of ground that supported only one by grazing." [5]

Unbeknownst to them, the ancient Irish farmers were helping their country as well as their own livestock.

The gorse also protected the land and the livestock in spirit. At the great festival of Beltane, gorse was the favorite decoration for the bonfires throughout Scotland and England, when all the Celtic lands celebrated the first day of Summer. Gorse was brought into the house to 'bring in the summer', and livestock would be herded between the great blazes fueled with gorse for purification and protection before being released onto the summer grazing. When this tradition diminished, torches of gorse and broom were still carried around the herds and farm buildings in order to cleanse the air and protect the animals against sterility. This had a practical effect as well: its decoction and its smoke were both effective insecticides, especially against fleas. [5]

Burning broom and gorse together also supplied a good alkali ash that served as a very nutritious fertilizer for refreshing the farmlands. [6] In some areas 'furze meadows' or 'gorse meadows' were intentionally grown up for a few years. They'd be pollarded (cut in half) for three years and used as animal feed, then burnt to the ground early in the year. Since gorse burns furiously and hotly when it is dry, doing the burning had some dangers, but all weed seeds in the ground were destroyed by the fire and the farmer was left with a richly top-dressed piece of farmland that was clean and ready for plowing. [7]

Gorse was prized for these gifts, and for its treasured ability to create a rich, stable and affordable yellow dye. [8]

Gorse is the fuel for the fire, and the feed that makes a horse run faster. Gorse is the cleansing that burns away impurity and the thorn that pricks us into motion. It is the fid of impetus, of energy, of going and doing and moving. It is also one of the favorite botanical symbols for Lugh Lamhfada, the shining prince of the Tuatha De Danann who ended the darkness in the land.

Long and long ago, the Tuatha de Danann, the Shining People, were at war. For seven years they had fought back the Formori and stopped them laying waste to the land. And for seven years, the Tuatha de Danann had planned. Now it was their time to act. Lugh Lamhfada, the brightest of the Shining People, began to gather the Tuatha clans to oppose the Fomorian army. Soon the Formori had found out their work. They rose like a wave to put down the Tuatha. The two armies agreed to meet on the field of Moytura.

On the night before the battle, the Tuatha de Danann made camp and readied themselves for the fighting. Gobhan, their great smith, checked and made ready the weapons. Dagda played his harp to bolster hearts. And the high king of the Tuatha de Danann, Nuada Airgetlam, saw to his men. Moving from tent to tent, his silver coronet shining in his dark hair, Nuada buoyed spirits and gave better weapons to the young men. Then he entered a tent where a young man with hair like gold was just lifting his sword from among the maps laid on his bed.

"Put your sword down, Lugh. You will not fight tomorrow."

Now Lugh was a brave man, and he grew angry at the words of his king. But Nuada held up a hand.

"Lugh, you are our best strategist and our greatest mage. I cannot afford to use you in the fray. You will stay in this tent, and as assurance you will have nine companions to guard you."

Lugh argued and stormed, but his high king had given an order.

In the morning, the Tuatha De Danann marched forth, and Lugh was left with his nine companions. On the other side of the field, the Formori marched out of their encampment. To attack the Fomorian host that day was to put your hand in a serpent's nest. At the head of their battalion marched Bres mac Elathan the traitor, Goll and Irgoll who had killed their father and eaten him, Omna and Bagna, sisters whose voices brought death. And the worst of them all was Balor of the Evil Eye, whose gaze brought death to all.

Sitting in his tent, Lugh heard the great cry as the battle began, and he tried not to think of his friends and kinsmen on the field. But his ears could not lock out the sound of the screams as warriors died, of the clash of armor and the singing of the lady Moriagan.

Lugh ground his teeth.

"Look out the tent and tell me how the fighting goes."

One young man looked out of the tent. "They are fighting so close that their feet are near touching, Lugh."

"But are we still holding?"

"We are."

Spears clattered as runners carried them to the fighting men. The sound of rattling chariot wheels clattered on the ground.

"Look out the tent and tell me how the fighting goes."

Another warrior looked out the tent.

74

"Oh, the battle's keen and sharp. The spears are red up to the butts, and our well of healing is filled with wounded men."

"But are we still holding?"

"Yes."

The battle raged on, the sound of it screaming through the air. And then there was a scream and a roar. Lugh jumped to his feet.

"Look out the tent and tell me how the fighting goes."

A young warrior looked out the tent, and turned back, white-faced.

"Oh Lugh, Balor has opened his eye! Our men are falling!"

Lugh's hands curled into fists.

"And I will not sit while my kin fall."

Quick as a flash, he became a hare and slipped out from under the tent flap, leaving the nine guards calling after him. He changed to his own form on the run, leaping into a waiting chariot. He rode into a battle with a charioteer's weapons; a spear, a bow and a sling. What he saw was terrible. Blood soaked the grass. Formori creatures ate from the bodies of the felled. The Tuatha men were few and far between. And here and there, great circles of men lay groaning and dying. Wherever Balor had been.

Lugh rode on. His arrows flew like sunbeams into the shadows, until they were gone. His spear flashed like lightning.

"Tuatha de Danann! To me!!!" he called. The men came together behind his chariot.

The Tuatha swept forward once more. Through the melee, Lugh rode, striking like lightning in all directions. His eyes were searching for the greatest foe.

And there, on the brow of the hill, he saw Balor with his aids. Two of them used sticks to raise the great eyelid of his one eye. Before him, men fell dead.

A wheel of the chariot was speared, and cracked. Lugh cut the horses loose and ran on. His spear cut and skewered. He had nearly reached the foot of the hill when his spear shaft snapped. But Lugh fought on, entering the empty circle beneath the hill. He was facing Balor.

"Hi!" he called, "Fat old man! There's been enough of you on this field!!"

A rumble of laughter came from the thing on the hill.

"And who are you?" the vile creature asked.

"A man who does not fear you." Lugh replied.

Balor laughed again "Lift up my eyelid, lads," he said, "so I may see the talkative fellow who is conversing with me." The lid was raised from Balor's eye. And that was when Lugh cast a stone from his sling. The stone flew so strongly that Balor's eye was pushed through Balor's brain and out the back of his skull. Now it was his own host that the dead eye looked upon, and their lines were falling as hundreds of Formori died. In that moment, the battle broke.

"Tuatha de Danann!" Nuada called out, "Let's have an end to it!"

And the Tuatha swept forward like a wave of clean water, and the Fomori were driven back and out of the land of Erin forever.

The lines of bright yellow blooms trace winding roads through the hills. Their scent hangs on the freshening breeze, coconut and vanilla mixed together. The weather is fine.

Follow the golden lines. Find out where they lead you.

Accept

Heather

An nì a thig leis a'ghaoith falbhaidh e leis an uisge.
What comes with the wind will go with the water.
-From *The Dindshenchas*

Botanical name: *Calluna vulgaris*
Family: Ericaceae
Ogham: Ur
Scots Gaelic: Froeach
Irish Gaelic: Froach
Welsh: Grug
French: Bruyère

Message: Learn acceptance. You cannot control all things that will come to pass. You can control how you will react to them.

An t-ór fe'n aiteann, an t-airgead fe'n luachair agus an gortafe'n bhfraoch.
Gold under furze, silver under rushes and famine under heather. [1]

This saying is still popular in County Kerry today, a poetic way to remember that soil bearing many heather plants will not be good. Heather promises hardship to the landholder. The scent of heather is the scent of damp earth and cold. It was described in the *Auraicept na n-Éces* as *silad clann*, 'clay of the Earth' and *uaraib adbaib*, 'the cold dwellings.' [2]

There are few sounds so evocative of barrenness as the rustle of a cold wind through the heather on the hill. It is the plant of grinding poverty and want.

And yet . . .

And yet the cold clay is where seeds sprout. It is white heather which blesses a bride with luck. It is the plant used as the badge of the proud mountain folk who hold their heads high. Few people would choose cold, wet and rocky land among the heather as their homes, but in these cold places of heather and rock, some of the greatest music and the strongest people in the British Isles grew to be great. They still thrive there today.

In past times, young heather shoots made the finest of beds, and their scent encouraged restful sleep. [3] Full of phenolic compounds, the plant also ensured a pest-free bedroom when used to make beds, brooms and scents for the home. [4] Tough as the Highland people themselves, heather stems were used in making farming tools and ropes as well. Heather is the earliest food of the year for wild deer and domestic sheep, green even when the snow lays on it in the highlands of Scotland, Yorkshire, and Northern Ireland. (5)

The plant was seen as valuable enough to be merited a position as one of the 'bushes of the wood' in the Brehon law, and clearing a field of it unlawfully earned the fine of a yearling heifer. (6)

It seems that what you see in the heather depends very much on what is within you. A tale from Munster tells us that to this day the grouse bird has been bemoaning its heathery lot in life for generations. Legend says its call is a complaint about High King Caoimh Duath, who decided the allotted nesting places for all birds in Ireland and Scotland. The grouse was given the heather of the hills, and today her descendants still cry:

Ó Caoimh, Ó Caoimh, Ó Caoimh cómhachtac!
Thug a'choill, thug a choill, thug a' choill dóibhsean,
agus an sliabh domhsa!
– Ó Caoimh, Ó Caoimh, Ó Caoimh, so strong!
You gave the wood, the wood, the wood to them!
You gave the heather to me! (7)

But resentment and suffering are not the only choice for those who endure hardship. It's said that in the 3rd century A.D., a daughter was born to the great poet Ossian. She was named Malvina, and she grew like a flower, slim and white as a swan. In the fullness of time she was to be married to her true love, Oscar the battle leader. But Oscar did his duty and went to battle for his king. He never came home. A messenger was sent to deliver the news. The messenger brought to the girl a spray of purple heather, much deeper in hue than most.

"He bled upon it as he died," the messenger said in sorrow, "and he asked us to bring it to you. His hearts' blood was always yours."

Malvina bowed her head and wept. As she cried, her tears washed the blood away, and with it, the color of the flowers.

Now Malvina had a touch of her father's magic. Seeing the flowers, she summoned what she could muster, and planted the sprig in the earth.

"There's been blood and tears shed on you already. Let those who bear white heather have neither bloodshed nor tears as their lot."

To this day, the carrying of white heather is a protection against the pains of the world. (8)

Heather, especially the white, is often worked into bridal bouquets. Even better for ending the pains of the world was making heather wine or heather-honey mead, said to make all hearts lighter. (8) Before the days of sugar cane, honey was the great sweetener of life, and hives that had been feeding on heather were among the most prized. Entire law tracts were devoted to these hives and how they should be cared for in Ireland and Scotland. (9)

When we see a field of heather, we look into a mirror.
Some of us will see poverty.
Some of us will see rocky ground and moan in despair.
Some will see the beauty of the purple blooms.
Others will listen to the buzzing of the bees and smile.

We may not always choose where we are standing. But what we see there is our choice.

Reflect

Aspen

M 'airiuclán hi Tuaim Inbir
ni lántechdais bes sestu
cona retglannaib a réir

Gobban durigni insin
conecestar duib astoir
mu chridecan dia du nim
is hé tugatoir rodtoig.

Tech inna fera flechod
maigen na áigder rindi
soilsidir bid hi lugburt
ose cen udnucht nimbi.

In Tuam Inbhir here I find
No great house such as mortals build
A hermitage, that fits my mind
With sun and moon and starlight filled

Twas Gobhan shaped it cunningly
This is a tale that lacks no proof
And my heart's darling in the sky
Lugh, he shaped the roof

Over my house rain never falls
There comes no terror of the spear
It is a garden without walls
And everlasting light shines here
-Sweeny the Mad, *Buile Suibhne*

Botanical names: *Populus tremula,* American species *Populus tremuloides*
Family: Salicaceae
Ogham: Edad
Scots Gaelic: Critheann
Irish Gaelic: Crann creathach
Welsh: Aethnen

Message: An action without a thought means little. Take time to reflect. Find a place of quiet. Allow yourself time and peace.

Aspen leaves in the wind are one of the most hypnotic sights in nature. They invite you to lie back, to watch, to let your mind wander as the leaves speak an unknown language with the wind.

Edad is the name of this fid, but no one today can be sure what the word signified to the people who first used it. Some link it to *eíth*, the sound of wind. Others connect it to *fi*, the aspen wand used to measure a corpse for burial. [1] Truth to tell, the word is as unknown to us as the whispers of the aspen.

Perhaps a few things we cannot readily name and pigeonhole are good to have in our lives. We must stop and study that which we do not know, and a time to pause is something we badly need at times. We live in a world that glorifies 'the hustle', and we have since the days when Calvin laid down his impossible standards for work and life. We glorify the process of pushing ourselves to the breaking point.

The problem is, we are breaking. Chronic stress causes our bodies to release hormones called glucocorticoids, as well as cortisol and adrenaline. [2] In small doses, these chemicals can save our lives, but when they are in our systems constantly, terrible damage is done. Our ability to sleep is destroyed. Our hearts are damaged. We raise our chances for a number of diseases, including diabetes, ulcers, and a wide range of mental illnesses. [3] And the suffering will not end if we allow it to get its claws into us: Several studies have shown that prenatal maternal stress has been linked to an increased risk of autism, depression, CEHD, schizophrenia, and reduced cognitive ability in children. [4] A study in 2010 showed that chronic exposure to a stress hormone causes modifications to DNA in the brains of mice, prompting changes in gene expression that were passed down to their offspring. [5] Stress can and will kill us. Yet we continue to laud the people whose faces are haggard with exhaustion.

What we have to remember is this: it's the poet who has taken the time to perfect their words who creates the finest work. It's the farmer considering their land carefully who brings in the best yield. In *The Triads of Ireland* we read these words:

Cetheora aipgitre báise: báithe, condailbe, imresan, doingthe

Four elements of folly: hasty deed, hasty judgement, hasty temper, hasty speech. [6]

When we look into the storytelling traditions of Old Ireland, we find again and again the hero who seeks the hermit for knowledge, the hero who retreats from the world in order to renew themselves and come back the better for it. Many things drive them to seclusion: grief, fear, curiosity, a love of the wild. At various times, many of the greatest figures in Irish myth sought solitude: Danu and Ogma, the Dagda and Dian Cecht, Fintan and Amergin, Finn and Ossian all had their time to seek the high hills and the quiet places. They may seem to be doing little, but what they learn in the wood enriches their community. Much can be learned in the quiet, and then much can be taught to others. This was true of Scáthach, the warrior woman who lived alone on the Isle of Skye and trained Cúchulainn in weaponry.

The aspen is one of the most flexible trees. It bends with the wind. Aspen suckers readily, forming stands of many trunks connected by a single root system. Individual trees are short lived: The grove allows individual stems to die and allows a new sucker to fill its place, growing from the roots. By renewing itself in this way, the aspen grove can live well into its thousands. [7]

When we take the lesson of Edad and renew ourselves as the aspen does, we can be as resilient. But when we refuse to take this lesson, it will eventually be forced upon us. Perhaps this is why one of the names for the aspen in the Ogham tract is 'Shelter of the Lunatic.' [8]

In the ninth century text, the *Book of Aicill*, we hear of a broken one who sought shelter in the wood. The text is *Buile Suibhne,* "The Madness of Sweeny". This is the tale we learn from it:

There was once a small king by the name of Suibhne, who ruled the area where County Louth is today in Ireland. An honorable man was he, though hasty in temperament and easily brought to passions of all sorts. But he was a good lord with a touch of the Sight, and was well able to think ahead and plan for bad harvests, bad weather and all manner of troubles. He was a good leader of his people, the Dál nAraide. Scottish originally, the Dál nAraide held territory through the Counties of Louth, Antrim and Down. Some said they had been there longer than the Fir Bolg.

Suibhne lived in good days, but all good times have their end. In the fullness of time, war came to the Dál nAraide. It came to pass that Congal Cáech, king of Ulaid, could stand no more the cruelties that his foster father, Ard Ri Domnall II, was laying the land under. Not only were his taxes high and hard, but Domnall was siding with the Christian clerics in banning the high holy days of Beltane, Samhain, Lughnasadh and Imbolc in the land. This Congal would not stand for, and neither would Suibhne. They agreed to fight at Magh Rath in 637 CE, but it was a terrible two-week battle. The lines of the poetry take us to that bloody field:

He made an onset on cruel Wednesday,
he wrought a harsh deed with horror:
so that by Congal Caech did fall
four score heroes by his hand.

He made an onslaught on dark Thursday,
so that defeat was wrought before his spearpoint:
and he slew fifty of the host,
that day he was no pitiable feeble man.

On Friday he set out.
It was a rare feat, it was a litter of wounds:
five score comely noble men,
wonderful was the round of wounds.

On Saturday to the battle came
Congal, before pursuing the spoil:
So that he slew a hundred famous nobles,
many were the lamentations for the dead.

For a blood-soaked week, brother fought brother and cousin fought cousin. There were good and honorable men in both factions. Some fought for their beliefs, some for the vow of fealty they'd taken to their high king. Both sides were right. Both were wrong. Both died.

In the thick of this terrible fight, it's said that Suibhne saw twin brothers slaughter each other on Sunday. The noise of kinsmen shedding one another's blood rang in his ears, deafening him. The horror of the drawn-out atrocity they were committing forced the king to his knees, for the greatest bond his people had, their lines of kinship, were being shredded before his eyes. It's said that while he sat, he saw a reflection in a pool of blood of his own body run through with a spear.
That was the moment when Suibhne broke. Screaming, he raced from the battle field, ripping off the clothes that bore the blood of kinsmen he'd slain.

The tale tells us his madness and his magic twined around one another, giving him the feathers of a bird. For seven years, he wandered alone.

Slowly, he came back to himself in the peace of the land, eased by the natural world. He spoke to one traveler of the peace he found in poetry:

"The bellowing of the stags
throughout the wood,
the climb of the deer-pass,
the voice of the white seas" [9]

In time, Suibhne Geilt, Suibhne the Mad, came to love the woods and their peace. He never truly returned to the world of men.

Suibhne's tale is a bittersweet warning. There is peace in solitude, but if we retreat forever, we help only ourselves. Suibhne healed, but he never led his folk again.

On the other hand, another noble can give us insight on the solitude we choose rather than that which we are forced into.

In 660 there was a king of Connaught named Guaire, and his best advisor was his half-brother Marbán. But Marbán did not sleep in his court. The other man had 'turned his back upon the world', as the Irish phrase is, and lived out in the wood. We are lucky enough to know this because a work was recorded and translated by Kuno Meyer in 1901 as "King and Hermit; a Colloquy between King Guaire of Aidne and his brother Marbán", being an Irish poem of the 10th century.

In this text, we learn of a king who, when he was weary of his work and his court, would seek his half-brother in his simple woodland home and stay for a time, calming himself and taking his ease with his dearest companion. There is a gentle teasing between these brothers that still rings true today: Guaire jokingly asks his brother:

Marbán, hermit,
Why will you not sleep upon the quilt I give?
More often you sleep stretched out,
Your head upon the pitch-pine floor.

Marbán replies:
I do not sleep upon a quilt
Though it might be for my health,
I find the restlessness of night
Shares with me better thoughts

The king comes to the hermit to refresh his soul many times, and his brother welcomes him again and again, easing his mind with the joys and the gossips of the wood where he lives:

A tree of apples - great its bounty!
Like a hostel, vast:
A pretty bush, thick as a fist, of tiny hazelnuts,
Branching, green.

A choice pure spring and princely water
To drink:
There spring watercress, yew-berries,
Ivy-bushes of a man's thickness.

Around it tame swine lie down,
Goats, pigs,
Wild swine, grazing deer,
A badger's brood.
A peaceful troop, a heavy host of denizens of the soil,
A trysting at my house:
To meet them foxes come,
How delightful!

Fairest princes come to my house,
A ready gathering!
Pure water, perennial bushes,
Salmon, trout. [9]

Whenever Guaire grows weary or sick at heart, Marbán will be there to welcome him with a quiet smile and a soft bed of rushes and heather.

Take an afternoon. Sit beneath an aspen tree. Watch his leaves flutter.

"There is time," he whispers, "time enough to sit and gossip with the wind. The time is there, if you choose to make it."

Let go

Yew

"O Cormac, grandson of Conn," asked Caibre,
"What is lasting in the world?"
"Not hard to answer," said Cormac,
"Grass, bronze, yew wood. That is all."
-From *The Counsels of Cormac*

Botanical name: *Taxus baccata*
Family: Taxaceae
Ogham: Edad
Scots Gaelic: Iubhar
Irish Gaelic: Iúr
Welsh: Yw
French: If

Message: There is a time for letting go. The end is not your enemy. Let go with grace.

Quiet yew trees stand in the rain, their needles shedding water on the graves in the churchyard below. This is a common sight throughout the British Isles. Melancholy, yes. But it has its place. There is a time for all things to pass. If the old does not pass away, the new cannot grow. No tree reminds us so well of this as the yew. It can live thousands of years, but not without change. Many times in its life, its central trunk will begin to rot. When this happens, a branch will put down a root into the decaying material at the center. In death, the new life of the yew is fed. This phenomenon is described as 'internal stemming' or 'internal rooting', and is as common in the yew species as breathing in the human. [1] In this way, the yew lives long beyond the years of most trees. Indeed, Thomas Laqueur writes: "The yew of legend is old and lays claim to immemorial presence. We are speaking here of two or three dozen exemplary giants, some with a circumference of ten meters, that have stood for between 1,300 and 3,000 years but also of many more modest and historically documented trees that have lived, and been memorialized, for centuries. At least 250 yews today are as old or older than the churchyards in which they stand." [2]

It is no wonder then that the tree is listed as 'the yew of resilience' in the *Carmina Gadelica*. [3]

In graveyards, the yew serves two purposes: they protect the dead, and their roots guide the traveling souls into the Land Under the Hill, where they will rest and be reborn. In this blessed twilight place, there is peace and plenty. [4]

When Christian and Pagan beliefs mixed, the folk under the hill became 'the Little Folk', ascribed by the Christian Irish as being the souls of honorable Pagans, too good for hell but too wild for heaven. In a way, their ancestors are still there, just a breath and a spadeful of earth away. [5]

The yew helped to fill the churchyards it guards as well. The earliest known wooden artifact is a yew spear, the Clacton Spear, found in 1911 at Clacton-on-Sea, in Essex. It is estimated to be over 400,000 years old. [6] The flexibility and durability of the yew tree have made it a preferred material for weapon-making through the centuries. The yew achieved notoriety in military history as the source of the renowned English longbow, the long range and deadly force of which helped win many battles for the English. [7]

For its beautiful, flexible wood, the yew was classed among the Nobles of the Wood in the Brehon law, a prince among trees and rightly so. Filled with the alkaloid taxine, it can kill a grown man in an hour. But Taxol, a derivative, can kill some cancers and save lives. [8]

In Old Ireland, life and death were parts of a whole. Death out of time was hard, but death was a step in life. The calf died to make cheese and vellum. The deer died to feed the people, and sometimes the hunter died in the chase. The warrior died to safeguard their folk. The salmon died when they were too old to avoid the net. The oath breaker died to restore the balance of the world and the safety of the community. Death in its proper place is a blessing, as we see in the Triads:

Trí báis ata ferr bethaid: Three deaths that are better than life:
bás iach, bás muicce méithe,   the death of a salmon,
bás foglada.   the death of a fat pig,
                            the death of a breaker of oaths [9]

The yew reminds us that death is a necessary passage into new life. Without the passing of the old, there cannot be growth. Without a note of sadness in the harpist's music, it will never be quite so sweet.

Today we see death as a hungry beast, an enemy and a failure of our skills. Better to see him as an old friend we're playing a game with. Eventually he'll win, but we will win often. Screaming at him only makes us sour. This is why the warriors were best respected when they faced death with a calm smile.

Perhaps none knew the balance of life and death so well as the Finna. They knew the joy of the fawn and the sweetness of the full-grown deer brought down in proud contest both.

Once as the Finna rested on the deer chase, a debate rose among them.

"Now what say you is the finest music in the world?" asked Osin, "Tell us that!"

"The cuckoo calling from the highest hedge," said his merry son.

"A good sound," said Finn.

"And you, Oscar?" Osin asked, "What do you say?"

"The highest music?" The battle leader shrugged. "It is the ring of spear on shield."

"That is a good sound," said Finn.

Now the others called out what they favored: The belling of a stag, the baying of a tuneful pack in the distance, the song of a lark, the laughter of a gleeful girl.

"Good sounds all," said Finn.

"And what say you?" asked Osin, turning to him. Wise Finn bit his thumb in thought.

"The best music?" said Finn, at last, "Why, the music of what happens. That is the best music."

Appendix A
References

Birch
(1) *Auraicept na n-éces: the scholars' primer; being the texts of the Ogham tract from the Book of Ballymote and the Yellow book of Lecan, and the text of the Trefhocul from the Book of Leinster* Calder, George, 1859-1941; Virgilius Maro, Grammaticus, 7th cent; Isidore, of Seville, Saint, d. 636, Published 1917, public domain
(2) *A Druid's Herbal of Sacred Tree Medicine*, Hopman, Ellen, Destiny Books, 1994
(3) "Silver birch: Betula pendula", Forestry Commission, https://www.forestry.gov.uk/fr/infd-8cykgl
(4) *Ogam: Weaving Word Wisdom*, Laurie, Erynn Rowan, Megalithica Books, 2007
(5) *Whispers from the Woods: The Lore and Magic of Trees*, Kynes, Sandra. Llewellyn Books, 2006

Rowan
(1) *Gods and Fighting Men: The Story of Tuatha de Danann and of the Fianna of Ireland*, Augusta, Lady Gregory, Harvard Press, 1905
(2) *A Druid's Herbal of Sacred Tree Medicine*, Hopman, Ellen, Destiny Books, 1994
(3) *Ogam: Weaving Word Wisdom*, Laurie, Erynn Rowan, Megalithica Books, 2007
(4) *Kindling the Celtic Spirit: Ancient Traditions to Illumine Your Life Through the Seasons*, Freeman, Mara, HarperCollins Publishers, 2000
(5) *Ortha nan Gàidheal: Carmina Gadelica*, Carmichael, Alexander (ed.), Edinburgh Press, 2006
(6) *Ogam: Weaving Word Wisdom*, Laurie, Erynn Rowan, Megalithica Books, 2007

Alder
(1) *The Poem-Book of Gael. Translations from Irish Gaelic Poetry Into English Prose and Verse*, Hull, Eleanor, Chatto & Windus, 1912
(2) *The Mabinogi and Other Medieval Welsh Tales*, Ford, Patrick K., Berkeley: University of California Press, 1977
(3) (4) *A Druid's Herbal of Sacred Tree Medicine*, Hopman, Ellen, Destiny Books, 1994
(5) *Ogam: Weaving Word Wisdom*, Laurie, Erynn Rowan, Megalithica Books, 2007
(6) *A Druid's Herbal of Sacred Tree Medicine*, Hopman, Ellen, Destiny Books, 1994
(7) *Ogam: Weaving Word Wisdom*, Laurie, Erynn Rowan, Megalithica Books, 2007

Willow
(1) *Silva gadelica (I.-XXXI.) : a collection of tales in Irish with extracts illustrating persons and places*, O'Grady, Standish Hayes, Williams and Norgate, 1892
(2) *A Druid's Herbal of Sacred Tree Medicine*, Hopman, Ellen, Destiny Books, 1994
(3) *Prehistoric woodworking from the Somerset Levels: 2. Species selection and prehistoric woodlands*, Orme, B. J., and Coles, J M., Somerset Levels Papers, vol. 11, pp. 7-24, 1985
(4) "Ancient wood, woodworking and wooden houses", Coles, J.M., EuroREA, 3/2006
(5) *Ancient Woodland. Its history, vegetation and uses in England*, London, Rackham, O., Arnold, 1980
(6) "Willow – Beauty and Spiritual Presence" Ireland Calling: http://ireland-calling.com/celtic-

mythology-willow-tree/

(7) *Ortha nan Gàidheal: Carmina Gadelica*, Carmichael, Alexander (ed.), Edinburgh Press, 2006

(8) *Beara: Dark Legends*, O'Sullivan, Brian, Irish Imbas Books, 2013

(9) *Ogam: Weaving Word Wisdom*, Laurie, Erynn Rowan, Megalithica Books, 2007

(10) *The Counsels of Cormac: an Ancient Irish Guide to Leadership: a New Translation from the Original Old Irish*; Cleary, Thomas, New York Doubleday, 2004

Ash

(1) *Whispers from the Woods: The Lore & Magic Of Trees*, Kynes, Sandra, Llewellyn Books, 2005

(2) *A Druid's Herbal of Sacred Tree Medicine*, Hopman, Ellen, Destiny Books, 1994

(3) "Why Other People Are the Key to Our Happiness", Markman, Art, Psychology Today, Jul 22, 2014

(4) "Cooperation and the Evolution of Intelligence", Proceedings of the Royal Society B: Biological Sciences, McNally, L, Brown, S.P., Jackson, A.L., DOI: 10.1098/rspb.2012.0206, 2012

(5) "Myeloid differentiation architecture of leukocyte transcriptome dynamics in perceived social isolation", Proceedings of the National Academy of Sciences of the United States vol. 112 no. 49, Cole, Steven W., et al.

(6) "Development of Brehon Law", Florida State Board of the Ancient Order of Hibernians, http://www.aohflorida.org/development-of-brehon-law/

(7) **Auraicept na n-eces : the scholars**' *primer; being the texts of the Ogham tract from the Book of Ballymote and the Yellow book of Lecan, and the text of the Trefhocul from the Book of Leinster*, Calder, George, 1859-1941; Virgilius Maro, Grammaticus, 7th cent; Isidore, of Seville, Saint, d. 636. Published 1917, Public domain

Hawthorn

(1) *Ogam: Weaving Word Wisdom*, Laurie, Erynn Rowan, Megalithica Books, 2007

(2) *A Druid's Herbal of Sacred Tree Medicine*, Hopman, Ellen, Destiny Books, 1994

(3) *Whispers from the Woods: The Lore & Magic of Trees*, Kynes, Sandra, Llewellyn Books, 2005

(4) The Plant Lore Archive, National Botanic Garden, Glasnevin, Dublin, August 2014

(5) "Fairy bush survives the motorway planners", Deegan, Gordon, The Irish Times May 29, 1999

(6) "Tree Lore: Hawthorn, The Order of Bards, Ovates and Druids", Freeman, Mara http://www.druidry.org/library/trees/tree-lore-hawthorn

(7) *A Dictionary of Irish Mythology*, Ellis, Peter Berrisford, Constable, London, 1987. (1st US edition from ABC Clio (hardcover) Santa Barbara, California, 1989

(8) "The Book of the Húi Maine", Royal Irish Academy, 2017 https://www.ria.ie/sites/default/files/mltheuerkauf_ui-mhaine_handout.pdf.pdf

Oak

(1) *A Druid's Herbal of Sacred Tree Medicine*, Hopman, Ellen, Destiny Books, 1994

(2) *Whispers from the Woods: The Lore & Magic of Trees*, Kynes, Sandra, Llewellyn Books, 2005

(3) (4) *The Hidden Life of Trees: What They Feel, How They Communicate*, Wohlleben, Peter. Greystone Books, 2016

(5) *Oak: The Frame of Civilization*, Logan, William B. W.W., Norton, 2005

(6) *Ogam: Weaving Word Wisdom*, Laurie, Erynn Rowan, Megalithica Books, 2007

(7) *Oak Trees Inside and Out*, Hipp, Andrew Rosen Publishing Group, 2004

(8) *An Oak Tree*, Byfield, Liz, Collins Educational, 1990

(9) *A Druid's Herbal of Sacred Tree Medicine*, Hopman, Ellen, Destiny Books, 1994

(10) *A Dictionary of Literary Symbols*, Ferber, Michael, Cambridge Press, 1999

(11) *The Poem-Book of Gael. Translations from Irish Gaelic Poetry Into English Prose and Verse*, Hull, Eleanor, Chatto & Windus, 1912

Holly

(1) *Talhaiarn; Thomas Oliphant Welsh melodies: with Welsh and English poetry*, Thomas, John, London: Addison, Hollier and Lucas, 1862

(2) *Pagan Christmas: The Plants, Spirits, and Rituals at the Origins of Yuletide*, Rätsch, Christian, Müller-Ebeling, Claudia, Simon and Schuster, 2003

(3) *Ogam: Weaving Word Wisdom*, Laurie, Erynn Rowan, Megalithica Books, 2007

(4) *Silva gadelica (I.-XXXI.): a collection of tales in Irish with extracts illustrating persons and places*, O'Grady, Standish Hayes, Williams and Norgate, 1892

(5) "Ilex aquifolium L", Journal of Ecology, Peterken, G. F., Lloyd, P. S., November, 1967

(6) *A Druid's Herbal of Sacred Tree Medicine*, Hopman, Ellen, Destiny Books, 1994

(7) *Trees in early Ireland*, Irish Forestry, Kelly, Fergus, http://www.forestryfocus.ie/wp-content/uploads/2013/02/Trees-in-Early-Ireland.pdf, 1999

(8) *Cath Maige Tuired: The Second Battle of Mag Tuired*, Gray, Elizabeth A., translator, Irish Texts Society, 1982

Hazel

(1) *The Trees of Britain and Northern Europe*, Mitchell, A. F., Collins, 1982

(2) "SELF Nutrition data, Nuts, hazelnuts or filberts", http://nutritiondata.self.com/facts/nut-and-seed-products/3116/2

(3) *Before Scotland: The Story of Scotland Before History*, Moffat, Alistair, Thames & Hudson, 2005

(4) *A Celtic Miscellany: Translations from the Celtic Literatures*, Jackson, Kenneth, Dorset Press, 1986

(5) *A Social History of Ancient Ireland: Treating of the Government, Military System, and Law; Religion, Learning, and Art ; Trades, Industries, and Commerce ; Manners, Customs, and Domestic Life, of the Ancient Irish People, Volume 2*, Weston Joyce, Patrick, Longmans, Green, and Company, 1903

(6) *Nature in Ireland: A Scientific and Cultural History*, Foster, John Wilson, Chesney, Helena C. G., McGill-Queen's Press, 1998

(7) "The Colloquy of the Two Sages", Stokes, Whitley, Revue Celtique 26, 1905

Apple

(1) *Ogam: Weaving Word Wisdom*, Laurie, Erynn Rowan, Megalithica Books, 2007

(2) *Kindling the Celtic Spirit*, Freeman, Mara, Harper Collins Publishers, 2000

(3) "Echtrae Chonnlai and the Beginnings of Vernacular Narrative Writing in Ireland: a Critical Edition with Introduction, Notes, Bibliography and Vocabulary", McCone, K., Maynooth: Department of Old and Middle Irish, 2000

(4) "Apple" Tree Lore, the Order of Bards, Ovates and Druids, http://www.druidry.org/library/trees/tree-lore-apple

Blackberry

(1) "Aidedh Ferghusa meic Léide: The violent death of Fergus mac Léti", Aodh Ó Dálaigh, transcribed, London, British Library, MS Egerton, 1782

(2) *Ogam: Weaving Word Wisdom*, Laurie, Erynn Rowan, Megalithica Books, 2007

(3) *A Druid's Herbal of Sacred Tree Medicine*, Hopman, Ellen, Destiny Books, 1994

(4) *Ireland's Wild Plants – Myths, Legends & Folklore*, Mac Coitir, Niall, the Collins Press, 2010

(5) *The Brehon Laws: A Legal Handbook*, Ginnell, Laurence, 1894

(6) *A Druid's Herbal of Sacred Tree Medicine*, Hopman, Ellen, Destiny Books, 1994

(7) *The Brehon Laws: A Legal Handbook*, Ginnell, Laurence, 1894

(8) (9) (10) (11) Williams, J. F. Caerwyn. Irish Literary History, Trans. Ford, Patrick K., University of Wales Press, English translation, 1992

Ivy

(1) *Poisonous plants in Britain and their Effects on Animals and Man*, Cooper, M. R., Johnson, A. W., Her Majesty's Stationery Office, London, England, 305 pp. Frohne, D., Pfander, H. J., 1983. A colour atlas of poisonous plants. Wolfe Publishing Ltd., London, England, 1984

(2) *Early Irish Farming*, Kelly, Fergus, Early Irish Law Series 4: 74-106, 1997

(3) *Ireland's Wild Plants – Myths, Legends & Folklore*, Mac Coitir, Niall, the Collins Press, 2010

(4) *A Druid's Herbal of Sacred Tree Medicine*, Hopman, Ellen, Destiny Books, 1994

(5) *Glamoury: Magic of the Celtic Green World*, Blamires, Steve, Llewellyn Worldwide Limited, 1995

(6) "The Holly and the Ivy (arr. J. Rutter)", Evanson, John, et al., The Holly and the Ivy, 2006

(7) *Mediæval Christmas Carols*, Ashley, Judith, Music & Letters, 65-71, 1924

(8) *Pagan Christmas: The Plants, Spirits, and Rituals at the Origins of Yuletide*, Rätsch, Christian, Müller-Ebeling, Claudia , Simon and Schuster, 2003

(9) *The Gardener's Guide to Growing Ivies*, Rose, Peter Q., Timber Press, 1996

(10) *Lebor gabála Érenn: The Book of the Taking of Ireland, vol. 6:*, Ó Riain, Pádraig (comp.), Index of names, Irish Texts Society 63, London: Irish Texts Society, 2009

Broom

(1) *British and Garden Botany*, Grindon, Leo H., 1864

(2) "Trees in early Ireland, Irish Forestry", Kelly, Fergus, Journal of the Society of Irish Foresters 56, 1999

(3) *Ireland's Wild Plants–Myths, Legends & Folklore*, Mac Coitir, Niall, the Collins Press, 2010

(4) *Food for Free*, Mabey, Richard, Collins Press, 1972

(5) *A Druid's Herbal of Sacred Tree Medicine*, Hopman, Ellen, Destiny Books, 1994

(6) *Flora of the County Dublin*, Colgan Nathanial, Hodges, Figgis & Co., Ltd., 1904

(7) *The Counsels of Cormac: An Ancient Irish Guide to Leadership*, Cleary, Thomas F., Doubleday Books, 2004

(8) *The Triads of Ireland*, Meyer, Kuno, ed. Vol. 13. Hodges, Figgis, & Co., Ltd., 1906

(9) "Bladud of Bath: the Archaeology of a Legend", Clark, John, Taylor & Francis, Ltd. on behalf of Folklore Enterprises, Ltd., 1994

Blackthorn

(1) *A Druid's Herbal of Sacred Tree Medicine*, Hopman, Ellen, Destiny Books, 1994

(2) *The Book of the Year: A Brief History of Our Seasonal Holidays*, Aveni, Anthony F., Oxford University Press, 2004

(3) *Trees and Bushes in Wood and Hedgerow*, Vedel, H; Lange, J., London: Methuen & Co Ltd., 1960

(4) "The Ancient Brehon Laws of Ireland", Gorman, M. J., Can. L. Times 20: 127, 1901

(5) *The Shillelagh Maker's Handbook*, Hurley, John W., Caravat Press, 2007

(6) *Irish Peasants: Violence & Political Unrest, 1780–1914*, Clark, Samuel; James S. Donnelly, University of Wisconsin Press, 1983

(7) "The stick is king: The Shillelagh Bata or the rediscovery of a living Irish martial tradition", Chouinard B.A., Maxime, http://www.cimande.com/blackthorn/pdf/stick_edited.pdf

(8) "Blackthorn", Woodland Trust, https://www.woodlandtrust.org.uk/visiting-woods/trees-woods-and-wildlife/british-trees/native-trees/blackthorn/

(9) "Roots of a Republic – An Irishman's Diary about Brehon tree law and the Irish National Foresters" McNally, Frank, Irish Times July 12 2017.

Elder

(1) *Trees and Bushes in Wood and Hedgerow*, Vedel, H. and Lange, J., p.196. Methuen and Co. Ltd, 1971

(2) "Mythology and Folklore of the Elder. Trees for Life: restoring the Caledonian Forest", Kendall, Paul., https://treesforlife.org.uk/forest/mythology-folklore/elder/, 2000

(3) *A History of Irish Music*, Flood, William Henry Grattan, Dublin: Browne and Nolan, 1906

(4) *The Counsels of Cormac: An Ancient Irish Guide to Leadership*, Cleary, Thomas F., Doubleday Books, 2004

(5) *A Glossary of Irish Slang and Unconventional Language*, Muirithe, Diarmaid Ó., Gill & Macmillan, 2004

(6) "The Contents of Later Commentaries on the Brehon Law Tracts", Simms, Katharine, Ériu 49: 23-40, 1998

(7) "The Puzzle of Blushing", Crozier, Ray, The Psychologist 23.5: 390-393, 2010

Gorse

(1) *Flora of the British Isles,* Clapham, A.R., Tutin, T.G., Warburg, E.F., Cambridge, p 331, 1962

(2) *The Brehon Laws: A Legal Handbook*, Ginnell, Laurence, 1894

(3) "On green and fodder crops not commonly grown which have been found serviceable for stock feeding", Darby, J., Journal of the Royal Agricultural Society of England, 2nd sers., vol.18, p.114-153, esp p.146-7, 1882

(4) "Furze: A Survey and History of its Uses in Ireland", Lucas, A. T., Béaloideas 1051, 1958

(5) *A Druid's Herbal of Sacred Tree Medicine*, Hopman, Ellen, Destiny Books, 1994

(6) *Farming in Ireland: History, Heritage and Environment*, Feehan, John, University College Dublin Faculty of Agriculture, 2003

(7) "Historical landscape studies in Ireland, with an appendix on the future of the Irish countryside", Simms, Anngret, Belgeo, Revue belge de géographie 2-3, 2004

(8) "Getting back to basics: transitions to farming in Britain and Ireland", Woodman, Peter C., 219-259, 2000

Pine

(1) "The Early Irish Linguist. An Edition of the Canonical Part of the AURAICEPT NA nECES. With Introduction, Commentary and Indices", Ahlqvist, Anders, Commentationes Humanarum Litterarum Helsinki 73: 1-81, 1982

(2) *Pagan Christmas: The Plants, Spirits, and Rituals at the Origins of Yuletide*, Rätsch, Christian, Müller-Ebeling, Claudia, Simon and Schuster, 2003

(3). *The Native Pinewoods of Scotland,* Steven, H. M., & Carlisle, A, Castlepoint Press, 1959, facsimile reprint 1996

(4) "Trees of Britain and Ireland", Milner, Edward, *Flora*: 15 and 120, 2011

(5) *A Druid's Herbal of Sacred Tree Medicine*, Hopman, Ellen, Destiny Books, 1994

(6) "Trees for Life: Species profile: Scots pine", https://treesforlife.org.uk/forest/mythology-folklore/scots-pine2/

(7) "Some cruxes in Críth gablach." Ó Corráin, Donnchadh, Peritia 15 : 311-320, 2001

(8) *Ancient Carpenters' Tools: Illustrated and Explained, Together with the Implements of the Lumberman, Joiner, and Cabinet-maker in Use in the Eighteenth Century*, Mercer, Henry C., Courier Corporation, 2000

Heather

(1) *Ireland's Wild Plants – Myths, Legends & Folklore*, Mac Coitir, Niall, the Collins Press, 2010

(2) **Auraicept na n-eces : the scholars' primer; being the texts of the Ogham tract from the Book of Ballymote** and the Yellow book of Lecan, and the text of the Trefhocul from the Book of Leinster, Calder, George, 1859-1941; Virgilius Maro, Grammaticus, 7th cent; Isidore, of Seville, Saint, d. 636. Published 1917, Public domain

(3) *A Druid's Herbal of Sacred Tree Medicine*, Hopman, Ellen, Destiny Books, 1994

(4) *Webb's An Irish Flora*, Parnell, P. and Curtis, T., Cork University Press ISBN 978-185918-4783, 2012

(5) Alice M. Coats, British Shrubs and Their Histories, London Press, 1964

(6) *The Brehon Laws: A Legal Handbook*, Ginnell, Laurence, 1894

(7) *A Tour in Scotland and Voyage to the Hebrides (1772)*, Pennant, Thomas, New Ed. Birlinn Ltd, 1998

(8) *Nature in Ireland: A Scientific and Cultural History*, Wilson Foster, John, Chesney, Helena C. G., McGill-Queen's Press, 1998

(9) *A Social History of Ancient Ireland: Treating of the Government, Military System, and Law; Religion, Learning, and Art; Trades, Industries, and Commerce; Manners, Customs, and Domestic Life, of the Ancient Irish People, Volume 2*, Joyce, Patrick Weston, Longmans, Green, and Company, 1903

Aspen

(1) *Ogam: Weaving Word Wisdom*, Laurie, Erynn Rowan, Megalithica Books, 2007

(2) *Coping with Stress, Health psychology-A Handbook*, Cohen, Bethany, and J. Williamson, Jossey Bass, San Francisco, 1979

(3) *Effects of chronic stress on dendritic arborization in the central and extended amygdala,* Vyas, Ajai, Savita, Bernal, and Sumantra, Chattarji. Brain research 965.1-2: 290-294, 2003

(4) *Perinatal environment and its influences on metabolic programming of offspring*, Tamashiro, Kellie LK, and Timothy H. Moran. Physiology & behavior 100.5, 2010,: 560-566

(5) *Epigenetic transgenerational inheritance of altered stress responses*, Crews, David, et al., Proceedings of the National Academy of Sciences 109.23, 2012,: 9143-9148, 2012

(6) *The Triads of Ireland*, Meyer, Kuno, ed. Vol. 13. Hodges, Figgis, & Co., Ltd., 1906

(7) *Trees of Britain and Europe*, Rushforth, K, Collins ISBN 0-00-220013-9, 1999

(8) *Ogam: Weaving Word Wisdom*, Laurie, Erynn Rowan, Smashwords Edition, 2011

(9) *Being the Adventures of Suibhne Geilt: A Middle Irish Romance*, Suibhne, Buile, Trans. and ed. *London*: Irish Texts Society, O'Keeffe, J.G., 1913

(10) *King* and Hermit: *A Colloquy between King Guaire of Aidne and His Brother Marban; Being an Irish Poem of the Tenth Century*, edited and translated by Meyer, Kuno, London: David Nutt, 1901

Yew

(1) *Ancient Trees: Trees that Live for a Thousand Years*, Lewington, A., & Parker, E., London: Collins & Brown Ltd., ISBN 1-85585-704-9, 1999

(2) "Beneath the Yew Tree's Shade", Laqueur, Thomas W., Paris Review, October 31, 2015

(3) *Carmina Gadelica: Hymns and Incantations Collected in the Highlands and Islands of Scotland in the Last Century*, Carmichael, Alexander, 1992

(4) *The Sacred Isle: Belief and Religion in Pre-Christian Ireland*, Dáithí Ó hÓgáin, Boydell Press, 1999

(5) *King of Mysteries: Early Irish Religious Writings*, Carey, John, Four Courts Press Ltd, 1998.

(6) *The Clacton Spear: The Last One Hundred Years*, Allington-Jones, Lu, Archaeological Journal 172.2: 273-296, 2015

(7) *The Yew Tree: A Thousand Whispers: Biography of a Species*, Hartzell, Hal, Hulogosi Communications, Incorporated, 1991

(8) *Yew*, National Non-Food Crops Centre, retrieved on 2009-04-23

(9) *The Triads of Ireland*, Meyer, Kuno, ed. Vol. 13. Hodges, Figgis, & Co., Ltd., 1906

Appendix B

Extant Manuscripts Concerning the Ogham and the Mythological Cycles Chronologically Listed

Note: Each of these books contains massive amounts of lore. Only the relevant texts are mentioned in this list. Accompanying them in each book are many other poems, later additions of fascinating Christian material, and general notes on Irish life and politics. Many of these texts are much older than their main sources: for instance, 7th century fragments of the Scholar's Primer exist, as well as 5th century pieces of the Triads. But the listed versions are the most complete sources, from which translations were created that I in turn used in this book.

Book of Leinster-12th Century
Containing:
I. *Lebor Gabála Érenn*, 'The Book of the Takings of Ireland'
II. *Táin Bó Cuailnge*, 'The Cattle Raid of Cooley'
III. The Metrical Dindshenchas
IV. Poetic treatise

Book of Ballymote-14th Century
Containing:
I. A copy of the *Lebor Gabála Érenn*
II. *Tecosca Cormaic,* 'The Counsels of Cormac' and other stories concerning King Cormac mac Airt
III. The Triads of Ireland
IV. Stories of Fionn Mac Cumhail and Brian Borumh
V. Rules on measures of Irish verse
VI. The only complete copy of the *Auraicept na n-Éces*, 'The Scholars' Primer'
VII. The *Lebor na gCeart,* 'Book of Rights' containing the Brehon Law

Yellow Book of Lecan-14th Century
Containing:
I. Rhapsody of the Irish prophet Bec mac Dé
II. *Cath Maige Rath* 'The Battle of Mag Rath'
III. *Bríathra Flainn Fhína maic Ossu,* 'The wise sayings of Flann Fína Or Aldfrith, son of Oswiu'
IV. Poem ascribed to Columcille
V. First rann by Mac Liag, bard of Brian Boru
VI. *Immram Brain maic Febail* 'The Voyage of Bran mac Febaill'
VII. *Táin Bó Cuailnge*, 'The Cattle Raid of Cooley'
VIII. *Togail Bruidne Da Derga* 'The Destruction of Da Derga's Hostel'
IX. *Suidiugud Tellaich Temra* 'The Settling of the Manor of Tara'
X. *Aided Con Roí* 'The Violent Death of Cú Roí'
XI. Clesa Conculaind 'The Feats of Cú Chulainn'
XII. *The Four Jewels of the Tuatha Dé Danann,* on the Tuatha Dé Danann and their magical education

XIII. *Tucait Fagbála in Fesa do Finn agus Marbad Cuil Duib* 'How Finn obtained knowledge, and the slaying of Cul Dub'

Book of Fermoy-15th Century
Containing:
 I. *Lebor Gabála Érenn*, 'The Book of The Takings of Ireland'
 II. The Fosterage of the Houses of the Two Milk Vessels
III. The Wooing of Emer
IV. The Adventures of Art Son of Conn
 V. The Voyage of Bran

Appendix C
Dates in Irish Myth and Legend

*Note: it is impossible to completely separate the Old Irish stories and beliefs from their later Christian additions, so I choose to record them as a whole rather than falsely show them as easy to separate. Also note that sources vary on many of these dates. What we are looking at is not a coherent whole, but an averaging of many sources in an attempt to see places where they all agree, which may be close to a truth. These dates are taken from a list compiled by Richard Marsh using the *Lebor Gabála,* The Annals of Ulster, The Annals of Clonmacnoise, The Annals of Tigernach, and Chronicum Scotorum. Myth Cycles noted.

The Mythological Cycle

3330 BCE – Destruction of the Tower of Babel

2956 BCE – Cesair, granddaughter of Noah, came to Ireland with 50 women and 3 men 40 days before the Deluge, landing in Cork. Only Fintan survived from this group through magical workings. He became the narrator of the Takings of Ireland.

2679 BCE – Partholon and his followers arrived. The Partholonians stayed 600 years; most died of the Plague.

2669 BCE – The Partholonians fought the Fomorians. Scholars today suggest they may have been mythologized from interactions with sea pirates.

2666 BCE – Slainghe mac Partholon is buried in Carn Slebhe Slangha (the Carn of the Hill of Slane)

2379 BCE – 9000 Partholonians died by Plague. Taimhleacht Muintire Parthalain marks their burial. (Tamhlacht = Plague Monument).

2349 BCE – The Nemedians come from Spain. Most died of the Plague or were killed by the Fomorians; 30 escaped.

1933 BCE – The Firbolg arrive. They divided Ireland into 5 parts.

1896 BCE – The Tuatha Dé Danann (the Tribes of the Goddess Dana) came from the northwest, bringing with them 4 great treasures. They had developed and practiced their magic arts in the North of Europe. They fought the Fir Bolgs near Cong, Co. Galway, and defeated them in the First Battle of Mag Tuireadh. The High King Nuada lost an arm in the battle.

1889 BCE – The physician Dian Cecht and the Smith Gobhan made a silver arm for Nuada.

1869 BCE – The Tuatha Dé Danann fought and defeated the Fomorians near Lough Arrow, Co. Sligo, in the Second Battle of Mag Tuireadh (known today as Moytura). Nuada was killed, and Lugh Lámhfada became king.

1829 BCE – Lugh established Aonach Taillten in memory of his foster mother, Taillte. Her burial mound is The Hill of Taillte, also called Taillten, in the townland of Teltown between Navan and Kells in County Meath.

1828 BCE – Eochaid Ollathair the Dagda becomes Ard Ri, High King.

1749 BCE – In the 80th year of his reign as Ard Ri, Eochaid died of a wound given to him at the Battle of Moytura. Eochaid is buried in the Brugh (Brú na Bóinne = Newgrange).

1748 BCE – Dealbaoith mic Ogma became king.

1728 BCE – Mac Cuill, Mac Cecht and Mac Greine began a shared kingship.

1699 BCE – The Milesians came from Spain and defeated the Tuatha Dé Danann at Tailltin. Their first battle was at Slieve Mis in County Kerry, where Scota, daughter of Pharaoh ben Mileach, died. She was buried between Slieve Mis and the sea. One of Ireland's early names, Scotia, honors her.

1698 BCE – The first Milesian kings, the brothers Eremon and Emhear, began a shared kingship.

The Ulster Cycle

1335 BCE – Ollamh Fodhla instituted the triennial Feis Tara.

658 BCE – Macha becomes queen.

128-114 BCE – Rule Of Eochaidh Airemh, brother of Eochaidh Feidhleach, husband of Étaíne.

107 BCE – Conaire Mor, son of Etersceoil, grandson of Étaíne, king.

38 BCE – Conaire Mor killed at Bruighin da Derg.

1 CE – Queen Maeve ascends her throne.

2 CE – Setena earns the name of Cuchulainn.

12 CE – The Cattle Raid Of Cooly. Cuchulainn and Maeve are both slain.

King Conor mac Nessa of Ulster died when he went mad on hearing about the crucifixion of Christ.

The Fenian Cycle

CE 12-157 – Rule of Conn *Céadcathach*, "of the Hundred Battles".

CE 140 – At the age of 17, Fionn mac Cumhail ended the Burning of Tara and became captain of the Fianna during Conn's rule.

CE 166-195 – Rule of Art mac Conn.

CE 227-266 – Rule of Cormac mac Art.

CE 268-284 – Rule of Cairbre Liffechair, son of Cormac mac Art.

CE 284 – Death of Fionn mac Cumhaill.

CE 284 – End of the Fianna at the Battle of Gabhra (Garristown, Co. Meath).

The Historical Cycle

CE 353 – Birth of Saint Patrick near Glasgow.

CE 364 – Saint Patrick captured by Irish pirates and brought to Ireland as a slave to tend pigs on Slieve Mis, Co. Antrim.

CE 369 – Saint Patrick released by an angel, studied under Saint Germanus on the Continent.

CE 432 – Saint Patrick arrived in Ireland as a bishop.

CE 433 – Saint Patrick built a fire on the Hill of Slane to challenge the druids of King Laeghaire at Tara.

CE 439 – Birth of Saint Brigit at Faughart.

CE 494 – Death of Saint Patrick. His tomb is in Downpatrick, Co. Down.

CE 520 – Birth of Saint Colmcille.

CE 524 – Death of Saint Brigit.

CE 593 – Death of Saint Colmcille.

These three saints are buried together.

CE 595 – Cumascach, son of High King Aedh Ainmire, killed by Brandubh, king of Leinster. This caused of the Battle of the Road of Dún Bolg the following year.

CE 596 – Death of High King Aedh Ainmire in the Battle of the Road of Dún Bolg.

CE 1198 – Death of Ruaidhri Ua Conchubair, Last high king of Ireland. Died near Lough Corrib, Co. Galway.

Source: Marsh, Richard, *Dates in Irish Myth and Legend*, https://www.legendarytours.com/dates.html, retrieved 4/20/2018

About the Author

Olivia Wylie is a professional landscaper who specializes
in the restoration of neglected gardens. In days of rain or snow she
creates works revolving around the connections between human and
green lives. She lives in Denver with a very patient husband
and a rather impatient cat.

www.ingramcontent.com/pod-product-compliance
Lightning Source LLC
Chambersburg PA
CBHW040255100426
42811CB00011B/1276